DATE DUE

SEP 18 1995	
JUL 16 1998	
MAY 06 2004	
MAY 15 2007	

DEMCO, INC. 38-2931

Anticipating Adolescence

ALSO BY H. PAUL GABRIEL, M.D.,
AND ROBERT WOOL

The Inner Child:
Understanding Your Child's Emotional Growth
in the First Six Years of Life

ANTICIPATING

How to Cope with

Your Child's

Emotional Upheaval

and Forge a

New Relationship

Together

ADOLESCENCE

H. Paul Gabriel, M.D.

Robert Wool

HENRY HOLT AND COMPANY

NEW YORK

Henry Holt and Company, Inc.
Publishers since 1866
115 West 18th Street
New York, New York 10011

Henry Holt® is a registered
trademark of Henry Holt and Company, Inc.

To protect the privacy of individuals, names and
details of cases have been changed.

Library of Congress Cataloging-in-Publication Data
Gabriel, H. Paul.
Anticipating adolescence: how to cope with your child's emotional
upheaval and forge a new relationship together/H. Paul Gabriel.
Robert Wool.—1st ed.
p. cm.
Includes index.
1. Parent and teenager. 2. Adolescent psychology. I. Wool,
Robert. II. Title.
HQ799.15.G33 1995 94-22591
649'.125—dc20 CIP
ISBN 0-8050-2373-9

First Edition—1995

Designed by Kate Nichols

Printed in the United States of America
All first editions are printed on acid-free paper. ∞

1 3 5 7 9 10 8 6 4 2

"Don't Need to Be a Rock Star to Feel Suicidal," letter to the Editor, *The New York Times*, April 11, 1994. Reprinted by permission of Elizabeth Freund.

Once again, for the three unique women
who inspired this book,
my daughters Vanessa and Zoë,
and their mother, Bridget Potter.

—R.W.

To those caring parents of my patients
who taught me how much they could help their children
when they understood them.

—H.P.G.

Contents

Anticipating Adolescence

1

An Introduction
to Adolescence:
Experiments and Upheaval,
but Not Hostility

Most parents anticipate with a shudder the years when their children will pass through adolescence.

They envision a time of explosive conflict, of continual turmoil between themselves and their children, with battles over everything from what clothes to wear and music to play, to which friends to have and what is appropriate sexual behavior.

But I have found, in my thirty years as a psychiatrist working with children and adolescents and their families, that this need not be a time of relentless warfare at all.

Indeed, I think there are widespread fears and misconceptions about adolescence, starting with the nature of the famous adolescent turmoil.

There certainly is turmoil. The years of adolescence, roughly the span between fourteen and twenty-one, perhaps longer, the time between childhood and adulthood, are years of enormous physical and emotional change and growth.

While such a degree of growth almost guarantees upheaval, it is important to understand that the struggle and turmoil are internal. The adolescent is wrestling with sudden exploding, disturbing emotions.

The great battle is not between adolescent and parents. Yes, there are outbursts, squabbles over differences that evolve from the adolescent's new feelings and attitudes. But the essential struggle is internal, a condition that is commonly overlooked, it seems to me, by parents who are anticipating adolescence, as well as those living through it.

At the same time, as a result of the inner upheaval, there is a huge amount of unpredictable outer behavior, part of the vast amount of experimenting, of testing out by the adolescent. Much of that behavior, often unexpected and disturbing to parents, is what gives adolescence a bad name. But that is how an adolescent naturally evolves, reaching out, gaining life experience, making mistakes, testing those hypotheses that are stewing in his mind.

So much of adolescence is what we call experiential, that is, based in experience. For example, as we'll see, the creation of self-esteem is critical to the adolescent's development. But this cannot be achieved simply by *thinking* about being more competent, more attractive, more intelligent. In a complicated process, the adolescent has the need to *feel* those qualities and knows that action must be taken to prove to himself that in fact he possesses all of those self-enhancing qualities. The more the adolescent registers success in an experimental action, the more he feels able to try other experiments. Thus self-esteem is a building process, building upon itself all the way through adolescence to adulthood.

For the adolescent, there is a new involvement with life. And his psychological being evolves from it, from these experiments with life.

The adolescent is, for example, very much concerned with sexual identity. Again, it is not enough for an adolescent boy to be aware of his new sexual maturity, his pubic hair, his larger penis, his new sexual fantasies of himself and Sharon Stone, or to merely think of himself as a heterosexual male. He has to test and prove it. He has to go out on dates, experience a certain amount of sexual experimentation and fumbling, take his sexual fantasies and translate them into experiential phenomena. It is out of that kind of behavior that his sexual identity becomes clarified. And that kind of behavior can be upsetting to parents.

The adolescent changes and so does his relationship with his parents. As we will see in the course of this book, the nature of this new relationship depends greatly on the parents and how they are psychologically capable of responding to their newly shaped child.

The process is not neat and predictable. Adolescents are not, for example, necessarily adversarial. Though so much has been written and portrayed about them suggesting that they are.

The course of adolescence is shaped jointly by children and parents, so it is critical that parents understand what their children are going through—but not expect that their children will. In this huge endeavor, it might help parents to know that the word *adolescence* comes from the Latin *adolescere,* which means "to grow up." And it will help if parents can remain aware that this is precisely the process their children are both suffering and enjoying, and to become sufficiently flexible to respond to it and to them.

Let's consider some of the principal developments of adolescence, both for children and parents, all of which we'll explore in this book.

THREE FORMS OF IDENTITY

When I counsel parents, I find it useful if they can understand that their adolescent is trying to establish three kinds of identity: self-identity, sexual identity, and role identity.

The great search for self

Working out her self-identity involves a series of separations from her parents. She is asking herself: "Who am I? What am I? What am I going to be?"

She is struggling to create herself as someone who can stand on her own, who is more and more independent of her parents. And, hopefully, her parents will be able to respond to this development, to gradually let go of their child who is becoming an adult. Ideally, her parents will be able to recognize that their role is to guide their child to the point where she can be independent of them, psychologically and physically, where she will be able to live apart from them, be involved intimately with another person, and be responsible for herself and her own life.

Throughout adolescence, the child is trying to announce, "I'm somebody special. I'm different. I'm independent."

She expresses this sentiment with three forms of emancipation.

The first often occurs before adolescence, at the tail end of the stage known as latency—around the age of ten—and extends into early adolescence. It is a symbolic statement and often surfaces with a new kind of clothing and music. "I wear my own stuff," she is saying, silently. "And I listen to my own sounds. . . . Ohmigod, your music is so boring."

There is no declaration or confrontation here, but a subtle statement that she is different and beginning to have different tastes. She isn't even aware of what she's doing or the symbolic statements she's making. Unconsciously, she's acquiring tastes from her peers and expressing them.

This might be accompanied by the first serious requests to stay up later. "I'm getting older," she reminds you, "and all my friends stay up till 9:30."

This kind of independence subtly creeps up on you. It's like what happens when you send your children away to summer camp and they come back after a month and appear to have grown a foot. They haven't, of course, and in fact, during the winter, they grew more, but you weren't aware of it.

So it is with the symbolic statements of independence. One day, when your child is twelve, she comes home with purple hair or asks for clothes you completely disapprove of. (And you can imagine how the nature of your response will affect the course of this development.)

And now, her statement is clear: "I'm totally different from you." Unconsciously, she has been building toward this point, acquiring the new accoutrements of her generation.

Next, her emancipation becomes conscious. She has a need to disagree, and she is aware of it. "Your politics are so reactionary, so conservative, I can't believe it. . . . I'm a radical. I'm cool."

An argumentative period evolves in which she makes an effort to prove that what is now is much better than what was then. It is a conscious effort to be different from you, and, once again, you can imagine the effect of your parental response.

The third form of emancipation, which is not so common, is a conscious act of rebellion from family tradition based on a need to break away from something she experiences as totally restrictive. It might not in fact be so restrictive, but that is how she perceives and experiences it.

I have seen this occur in religious families where, for example, an adolescent son decided he was prohibited from dating a girl of a different religion. He wasn't, though it was clear that his orthodox Jewish father did prefer that the young man socialize with Jewish girls. The result was a rupture in the family, constant screaming and yelling, indeed the kind of open turmoil that so many parents assume is typical for adolescence.

As I said, this open, vocal, destructive rebellion is in fact rare. Normally, the real fight is going on inside the adolescent's head, and normally it remains there, if parents are able to handle the adolescent's demands of emancipation with some discretion, empathy, and understanding.

Is life really going to disintegrate if your child has purple streaks in her hair?

The impact of puberty and a new sexual awareness

Puberty brings physical and biological changes, by which the child in many ways grows into adulthood, adding inches, pounds, and, most significantly, developing sexually.

The schedule of events in puberty varies for each individual. It starts around age nine for girls, and it proceeds about two years faster for a girl than a boy. In addition to adding height and weight and fullness to the hips, a girl begins to develop breasts and pubic hair. Then, between the ages of eleven and fifteen, she begins to menstruate. Her ovaries, fallopian tubes, and uterus have been growing, and with the onset of menstruation, she is capable of becoming pregnant.

A boy starts growing later than a girl, but he adds inches at a faster rate and by the age of fourteen or fifteen he is normally taller and more muscular than a girl. Somewhere between the ages of ten and thirteen, a boy's testicles and the sack that holds them, the scrotum, become larger. Pubic hair appears, and his penis grows. Then he is capable of ejaculation, indicating that there is enough testosterone in his body to produce sperm, his symbolic counterpart of the girl's menstruation. Typically, he discovers this new development through "wet dreams" or masturbation.

For both girls and boys, this is a huge amount of growth, change, and development in a few years. They try to process, integrate, understand, and accept everything that is happening to them, but much of it is quite confusing, threatening, and upsetting. It is critical that parents be aware of the impact of this process.

To further complicate the adolescent's life, psychological adolescence does not correlate with physical adolescence. A young man may have the body of a professional wrestler, but his mind is still that of a twelve-year-old. A thirteen-year-old girl may have the physical development of a twenty-five-year-old woman, but her psychological development is still that of a young adolescent.

For the first time in their lives, these girls and boys are capable of adult sexual activities. And they have the normal curiosity and hormonal urges to try them out.

From a Freudian perspective, these developments lead to adolescence as a time for reworking the Oedipus complex, and can also be considered another aspect of the adolescent's quest for self-identity.

Here is a greatly oversimplified account of the Oedipal complex: Roughly between the ages of three and five, the male infant, quite unconsciously, finds himself erotically attracted to his mother, jealous of and competitive with his father. However, if the child's development is healthy, he reaches a point where he accepts the futility of his sexual fantasies about his mother and replacing his father, indeed fears that such yearnings could lead to castration, and begins to emulate his father instead. If the infant is not allowed or able to work through his Oedipal conflict, his sexual attachments will be neurotically affected in later life.

The theory, as Freud himself admitted, unraveled somewhat with girls, but the idea was similar. The girl separates from her maternal attachment, has sexual fantasies toward her father, and finally abandons those longings for him.

While the theory in general and its application to adolescents are much debated, by becoming familiar with its essential elements you can better understand what your adolescent is going through.

Unquestionably, one form of the adolescent's separation from his or her parents is sexual. If he is going to respond to the new biological, hormonal urges of normal adolescent development and forge new sexual relationships, the normal relationships of the adolescent years, he is going to have to sever his infantile sexual ties.

In Freudian terms, he will have to abandon his parents as infantile sexual objects, as providers of physical satisfactions like eating and touching, and take on new, real sexual objects. He will have to respond to the incest taboo and give up the forbidden, at the same time discovering the pleasures of new personal and love relationships.

This is different from the Oedipal evolution between the ages of three and five. Now, he has a sexual capacity of his own, and he can recognize his own parents as sexual creatures. Now, the forbidden, unconscious incestual urges are accompanied with a new element of reality. That can be very confusing and frightening to the young adolescent. Usually, he will be able to make this transition and give up the forbidden without being so shaken and traumatized that he becomes incapable of forming new relationships.

Once again, all of this happens unconsciously and with considerable inner confusion. It's another stormy state that may well be reflected in the adolescent's attitude toward his parents.

The sexual activities of adolescents are notorious, of course, and perhaps the greatest source of tension between children and parents, as we will explore later in this book. Ultimately, those activities are part of the internal process and the external experimentation that enables adolescents to become relatively comfortable with all of their sexual changes and maturation, and to be able to establish their sexual identity.

In other words, around the age of sixteen to eighteen, the young man is finally able to say to himself, "Okay, I know who I am sexually, and what I can do with the opposite sex. I'm a man.

That's what I am." And he, with some awareness of his differences from a woman, feels reasonably comfortable with that.

The young woman reaches the point where she can say, "I am a sexually functioning woman. That's what I am." And she, aware of her differences from a man, feels reasonably comfortable with that.

Or the adolescent decides he or she is homosexual, a realization that usually brings special complications. But this, too, is a form of sexual identity.

A role in society

The attainment of role identity usually signals the end of adolescence. It marks the time when an adolescent finally sees with some clarity her role in society and in our culture. Like self-identity and sexual identity, role identity is realized only after years of testing and feeling, which means it might be reached anywhere between the ages of eighteen and thirty.

That might seem at first like quite a stretch for the period of adolescence, even an insult—as if some particular adolescent can "never seem to grow up." But bear in mind that an adolescent might, for example, need all the years of graduate school, and perhaps additional specialized training, to reach that point in life where he or she feels comfortable with her vision of her role.

Or if college or graduate school are not part of her plans, it might take this long simply to reach maturity. The concept of role identity derives from Erik Erikson's masterful book *Young Man Luther*. In this brilliant psychoanalytic consideration of Martin Luther's life, Erikson noted that Luther was thirty before he was able to break away from his symbolic father, the Pope, and define his own role in life, that of reformer of the Roman Catholic Church.

As I said, years of testing, feeling, thinking it over, fantasies wrestling with realities. An eight-year-old might announce that when he grows up, he intends to be the shortstop for the Boston Red Sox. But by age twelve, he has played enough baseball to have tested that idea and role. He knows and silently admits to himself that though he might be a good enough shortstop to play for his Little League team, he's simply not going to make the bigs, he's simply not ever going to be good enough to play for his beloved Red Sox.

But with that sad discovery and admission, he has freed himself to consider other roles. And throughout adolescence and young adulthood he continually tries them out. Doctor? Editor? Entrepreneur? Perhaps he comes to realize that he isn't that interested or good enough in the sciences, so maybe the idea of being a doctor is not such a great one. Meanwhile, serving as an editor on the high school, then college literary magazine was interesting, even though the fit was not completely comfortable. But working as the publisher of the college magazine was intriguing; conceiving new ways the magazine could be sold—the special supplements that brought in so much extra income—was a really engaging and extremely satisfying job.

And so the role evolves.

For some, the recognition of one's role in life comes earlier than for others. A blue-collar worker on an automobile assembly line might begin that kind of work on finishing high school, at the age of eighteen or nineteen, often following a family pattern. Soon he feels certain that this will be his life's work. This will be his role.

A white-collar worker reaches a similar conclusion a bit later, after college, at twenty-two or twenty-three years of age. I am an art director, she says, feeling and envisioning her career and role.

The professional, however, might not be able to make such a statement until the age of thirty, when graduate school or residency is completed.

But after all the testing and the experiential data are gathered and internally processed, there is finally a resolution of role identity. And with that, role identity becomes incorporated with individual identity, that first separation from the parents, as well as with sexual identity. At that point, the individual has achieved overall identity.

A DIFFICULT CHALLENGE

I noted that the essential adolescent turmoil is internal, that the familiar picture of perpetual screaming and pitched battles between parents and children is something of a myth.

This is not to suggest that these are years of great calm. They can't be. Not with your child passing through all the momentous stages of physical and psychological growth and change mentioned above. Not with the vast amount of vital, often unpredictable experimental behavior that is linked to the inner psychological developments.

Even without tumult, this evolving, shaken child can be a difficult challenge for a parent to understand and, at times, to live with. Anna Freud, daughter of Sigmund and an early leader in psychoanalytic work with children and adolescents, provides a useful description in her seminal book *The Ego and the Mechanisms of Defense.*

Adolescents are excessively egoistic, regarding themselves as the centre of the universe and the sole object of interest, and yet at no time in later life are they capable of so much self-sacrifice and devotion. They form the most passionate love-relations, only to break them off as abruptly as they began them. On the one hand they throw themselves enthusiastically into the life of the community, and, on the other, they have an overpowering longing for solitude. They oscillate between blind submission to some self-chosen leader and defiant rebellion against any and every

authority. They are selfish and materially-minded at the
same time full of lofty idealism. They are ascetic but will
plunge into instinctual indulgence of the most primitive
character. At times their behavior to other people is rough
and inconsiderate, yet they themselves are extremely
touchy. Their moods veer between light-hearted optimism
and the blackest pessimism. Sometimes they will work
with indefatigable enthusiasm and at other times they are
sluggish and apathetic.*

That narcissistic quality she refers to is just one characteristic
that can make life difficult. That self-centeredness continually
gets translated into such ideas as "nobody ever felt the way I do.
Nobody sees the world the way I do. Nobody has as urgent a need
as I do." In other words, the whole world depends on attending
this particular party, or going on this particular trip, or buying
this particular sweater.

The narcissism can lead to a sense of omnipotence, the idea
that "nothing bad can happen to me." This false sense of power
clearly affects judgment, for example, when it comes to driving.
And accidents, including automobile accidents, are the single
largest cause of death in youths.

As a parent, you may be faced with this omnipotence as you
try to reason with your child about the sensible use of a car, or the
precautions to be taken with sex.

As Anna Freud's description suggests, there is also a mer-
curial quality about adolescents. Peter Blos, perhaps the leading
psychoanalytic theorist on adolescents, captures this quality in
his book *On Adolescence* with his engaging idea of the "rescue
fantasy":

*The Ego and the Mechanisms of Defense, by Anna Freud; translated from the German
by Cecil Baines. New York: International Universities Press, Inc., 1946; Third
Printing 1950, pp. 149–50.

The adolescent and post-adolescent expects a solution to a conflict by a change to a beneficent environment . . . the expectation to be rescued by a person, circumstance or privilege, or good luck. . . . If only I had a different job, if only I were married, if only I could live in Europe, the East, the West, the country, the city. If only I had a different name, were two inches taller, and so on. [It is] a reduction of intricate problems to a single condition on which everything seems to hinge.*

Indeed, the rescue fantasy would seem to be a phenomenon that we all experience long past adolescence. But as a parent trying to get your adolescent to confront a difficult problem, you can imagine the effect of the rescue fantasy on the youngster's thinking.

THE IMPORTANCE OF PARENTAL ACCEPTANCE

Ultimately, the course of the adolescent years depends greatly on how you as a parent respond to your admittedly challenging child. Can you accept in your child a certain amount that has become different from yourself? A certain amount of emancipation? A certain amount of her blatant effort to be unique? Can you accept that the time has arrived when you can no longer rule by edict?

I often find parents engendering rebellion in their children by taking absolute positions, commonly over nonissues. And often I find parents locked in struggles with their adolescents where it is

On Adolescence: A Psychoanalytic Interpretation, by Peter Blos. New York: The Free Press, A Division of Macmillan Publishing Co., Inc., 1962, p. 154.

not the issue that really matters but the question of who has control.

After all, what harm comes to a child because she likes loud rock music? Or is momentarily taken by purple hair? Or denounces your brand of politics?

On consideration, I'm sure you'll agree that none of these typical issues of emancipation needs to become a battleground. This is not to say that you are supposed to stifle your own opinions. Or that you can't try to talk your child out of the purple hair. Or that you have to abandon your own rights. There is no need for you to suffer rock-and-roll blasting through your home: "Please, play your music in your room, and please keep the volume down."

Nor am I suggesting that you abandon your role as a parent. Music may not be dangerous to your child, but drugs, alcohol, smoking, or casual sex can be. Those you must argue firmly against, continually remembering that a prohibition is not enough; you must also try to educate, reason, and influence.

The role of a parent changes. You are no longer dealing with the infant whom you can simply pick up and carry to a safe place if she doesn't respond to your request. Nor are you dealing with the compliant child of the latency years prior to adolescence, a child who has a strong desire to please her parents. Now you are confronted with a child who is getting far too big to be carried, who wants profoundly to separate from you, to find her new self in the midst of numerous internal upheavals.

Confronting and trying to guide this new child of yours can be frustrating and confusing. Frequently, you will find yourself angered, upset in some internal way by some statement or action of your child. Frequently, your child will trigger in you some emotion that relates not so much to the moment, the event you two are discussing, or the argument you two are having, but to some moment from your own past.

In psychoanalysis, this phenomenon is known as "countertransference." It occurs when the patient, through statements or actions, stimulates emotions in the therapist. At times, these responses of the analyst are inappropriate to what the patient is saying or doing. And such responses can distort, even destroy, the analytic treatment. In a sense, these are problems that the therapist has, not the patient; the patient merely triggers them. Well-trained therapists are alert to such countertransferential flashes and developments, able to recognize them and analyze them. Many of them have gone through their own psychoanalysis in order to cope with just such developments. They are able to keep them from derailing the process of the therapy.

To some degree, you will have to do the same with your child. When a statement from her about the clothes you wear, for example, suddenly enrages you, what is that really all about? Surely, you can grasp intellectually that such an attack is a reflection of your daughter's changing taste, of her efforts to show you how she is different from you. Maybe it's also a flash of anger from her, a way of attacking you for any number of grudges she is harboring. To be sure, you can live without her telling you how to dress, but generally, you are able to maintain a perspective on such remarks which she cannot yet possess.

Yet you find yourself lashing out at her, becoming suddenly overcome with anger. To whom is that anger really directed? What does her attack on your style really represent to you? Is this the kind of criticism you suffered from your own mother, a painful attack on your self-esteem that you are reliving? Are you sensitive to the remark because of a present-day concern that you are not looking the way you like, not feeling so good about yourself, your body image, while your daughter is looking better and better, with a freshly nubile body that on some level reminds you of what your own body no longer is?

The possibilities are nearly endless. Whatever the source of your sudden, unexpected, puzzling response to your daughter, you have to think about it. Not everyone can self-analyze themselves. But like a good therapist, you can be on the alert for such responses. And you can make the effort to control them.

Bruno Bettelheim, who did such important work with psychotic and other profoundly disturbed children, analyzing their problems, training and educating them so they could become functioning adults, offers a wise suggestion: try to empathize with your child, try to recall what life was like when you were a teenager. If you can put yourself in her place, you may be able to understand her much better.

That is a wonderful idea, but unfortunately, in my experience at least, not everyone can, for whatever psychological reasons, recall adolescence. Still, empathy is worth a try, and even if you don't succeed, Bettelheim's idea and your efforts will move you closer to what I think is at the heart of an adolescent experience that is both healthy and comfortable for you and your child—a climate of negotiation.

A TIME FOR COMPROMISE

Increasingly, adolescence will be not only a time when you cannot rule by edict but a time when you cannot exactly win, only compromise.

This is a difficult concept for many parents to accept, but it is the reality. With some issues, there will be no outright winners. Parents who cannot live with this change become rigid and issue angry declarations. "You can never . . . ," they proclaim, but as soon as they utter the word *never,* they have created an issue around which the adolescent's struggle for independence begins to crystallize.

Can you prohibit your child from doing what is socially acceptable by her peers and their parents? Only at a terrible price.

You can, however, negotiate a compromise with your daughter that allows the two of you to proceed with life and perhaps, through the very act of compromise, to feel better about each other and closer to each other.

Take the telephone as an example. Adolescents, especially adolescent girls, discover the phone, and it soon becomes part of their anatomy. The next step is for them to request or demand a phone in their room. When that issue came up in a colleague's family, there was much passionate discussion and hand-wringing. Their daughter was only twelve, but she argued that all her friends had phones *and* TVs in their rooms. Calls to a handful of parents confirmed the girl's claim, but that still left my colleague and his wife with a difficult decision. They felt that their daughter, with a phone behind the closed door of her room, would never get off the phone. She was at a point in school where her homework was increasing and becoming more important. So they were doubly concerned that she would not do her homework and that they would have to continually police her to be sure that she did.

They told her exactly what they were worried about and that they were wiling to give her a phone for six months, on a trial basis. If, during that time, she could show them that she could control the time she spent on the phone so that it did not interfere with her homework, they would be willing to let her keep the phone in her room.

The girl was disappointed, but accepted the compromise and the challenge. In her own way, she balanced the calls with her work, and six months later, the parents let her keep the phone, warning her that if they found themselves becoming phone police, out it would go.

My friends might have easily dismissed their daughter's plea. She was simply too young for her own phone, they might have reasoned, and besides, neither of them ever had a private phone when they were growing up. But dismissal would have been an emotional blow for her. It would have meant that her parents didn't respect her.

Instead, they listened and heard something in her passionate argument that they had not known: her peers had phones. They addressed this situation yet never abandoned their own parental concerns. They showed her respect by explaining themselves, by giving her rational reasons for their position.

This story demonstrates some of the attitudes and behavior that become increasingly necessary for both parent and adolescent to adopt: they must respect each other and listen to each other, be willing to agree to disagree, and not let the disagreement fester or escalate. So each person can say whatever he wants about the other's taste in music, for example, and find a way to live with the differences that is comfortable for all parties. It means respecting each other's differences.

If you and your child have such an understanding, you will be able to defuse potentially explosive situations. You will be able to talk to each other.

Talking to each other is critical—and not always easy. There will be times when you will want to talk, perhaps when you sense something meaningful has happened at school, or with his friends, and he will be absolutely prickly. "Nothing is going on," you will be informed. Or "I really don't want to talk about that now."

Such a reaction is often a reflection of his unconscious reaching for independence. Whatever is bothering him, he is saying, he can handle it. Try to persist. Not bludgeon, not demand, but empathetically persist. Being sensitive to his personality in general, his mood in particular, keep trying, as difficult and irritating as it might be. The more you do, the more you will learn the secrets of getting him to open up to you.

For example, you can figure out when he's most likely to talk. One mother told me that the easiest time for her to talk with her son is when they are walking. She has no idea why this is such a good time for a talk, but whenever they head out together, she carries a secret agenda of topics.

Perhaps one of the reasons is that during those walks her son does not feel the pressure and anxiety of "a talk." He does not unconsciously feel as if he will have to defend himself.

Try not to make every discussion a summit. Often a short exchange in passing will provide important information and clues, reveal a particular anxiety or problem that, once revealed, can be pursued later on.

Try to persist, expect frustration, and be tireless. It really is the only way, and it is entirely worth the effort. Otherwise, you may eventually find that you and your adolescent no longer have any regular meaningful communication, in which case you become less parent and adolescent than related strangers sharing a home.

Above all, don't fear argument. Welcome it. So often what looms as a monumental confrontation quickly deflates into a sincere, meaningful exploration.

One friend, now the mother of an adolescent and a younger child, told me, "My father was always available for me to argue with." Her father, whom I knew, was a somewhat conservative, older European gentleman who had difficulties with the world his daughter was growing up in, especially with the relative looseness of its social mores as compared with his own. But he was wise enough to know that he could not impose his views arbitrarily on his daughter, that he had to try to reason with and convince her. And in many ways, she readily admits, he did.

One of their biggest differences was over which college she would attend. In the end, she chose a fine school, even though he was trying to persuade her to select another one, closer to home, which is often a dividing point on this issue.

I recall a case in which a parent could not accept a child's choice of college, as respectable as the school was. So he used his ultimate weapon, his atom bomb. He refused to pay unless the child agreed to the parent's choice.

I couldn't convince him of the error of his way. He would surely win a battle but lose the war. He would force his child to go to a particular college, but he would lose the child. And he did: before a year was up, the child had left school, found a job, and removed herself from the orbit of the family.

Not surprisingly, this was a family where there was precious little real communication between parents—especially father— and adolescent daughter. Instead of communication, an attempt at understanding and compromise, there was fairly unbending parental authority. But as I noted, the days when parents give all the orders and the child is expected to submit are well over when the child reaches adolescence. Parents who won't or can't recognize the change stand a good chance of accomplishing what that father did—physically and emotionally losing their child.

2

Latency: One Last Chance

The years of latency, from seven to ten, have been characterized since Freud as a time of relative calmness, a respite between the early years of infancy and basic personality development and the great upheaval of adolescence.

Latency, in fact, is a time somewhat neglected by psychologists. But for parents, it is a most important stretch. In a way, it may be viewed as a last chance for parents to lay the groundwork for adolescence.

It is a time when parents, if they haven't already, can begin to treat their children as real people. This means listening to them with new attention and respect and so creating the kind of foundation upon which negotiations can be developed. And it is during latency that the first negotiations of independence will normally take place.

It is also a time when limits on behavior can still be set. Children of this age are strongly driven to please their parents and will respond to limit setting in order to please. These same limits will provide issues around which appropriate and meaningful negotiations of adolescence can subsequently occur.

Further, it is a time to build trust. I believe it is possible for parents to develop trust and have it grow, like money invested in a fund, so it will be available when it will certainly be needed in the adolescent years. If trust has been established, your uncertain, experimenting adolescent can feel it's safe to turn to you for guidance, to pause and listen to you.

Let's examine these and other significant characteristics of the latency period.

THE SHIFT BEGINS: LISTENING

Until your child was seven, it's fair to assume, you unconsciously perceived her as a kid, a little, lovable, sometimes exasperating, often funny kid. Your basic role was that of protector and provider. There was not a lot of give-and-take in life. She had requests, of course, but you decided what was acceptable and allowable. There was little discussion and no negotiation over anything serious.

With latency, this attitude should begin to shift. You will start to see the first signs of separation, of being slightly different, of that search for independence that will become so vivid in adolescence. And those early strivings should be recognized and respected.

The issues she raises, for example, might still at first seem slightly comical to you, but they bear a new importance for her. Laugh them off, and your child will begin to feel diminished, and also that you're not someone she can talk with—two feelings that could be extremely damaging if carried into adolescence.

But if instead you begin to listen to her—flawed logic and magical thinking included—and respond to her as you would to an adult, your relationship will move to a new level.

Listening in this manner does not necessarily mean agreeing. You do not stop being a parent and making decisions the child is still not capable of making. It does, however, mean giving reasons why you disagree.

And it does mean that you are genuinely open to argument.

I am reminded of an argument over summer camp that occurred in the family of some friends of mine. Their eight-year-old daughter had begun a campaign to go to sleep-away camp, as her ten-year-old sister did. In fact, she had visited her sister at camp the summer before and decided that it was the best place in Maine, if not the world.

My friends agreed that their younger daughter was ready for a month of camp, and that the camp in Maine would be fine. They already knew it was a good, caring place, and life would probably be a bit easier if both children went to the same camp.

Then their older daughter spoke up. She had a lot of trouble with that plan, she said, and wanted a hearing. It was scheduled for dinner that night.

Actually my friends were quite skeptical. They were willing to give their older daughter a chance to present her case, but their minds were pretty much made up.

To their surprise, her arguments were so logical and powerful, they had to change their minds. The camp, she said, was a place she had found and chosen on her own. It was her place, and she had grown to love it as her place, her turf. If her sister went there, it would be one more thing she had to share (and compete over) with her sister, and that simply wasn't fair. Going to camp had been a great experience for her, she said, and she thought it would be for her sister as well. But, she pointed out, her sister didn't have to go to the same camp. After all, she reminded her parents, Maine was full of camps. Her sister could simply go to one of those.

The arguments were cogent and compelling. My friends could grasp what the camp meant to her and understand how the issue of sibling rivalry came into play. They also knew that going to this camp had been her first experience at real separation, that it had taken a lot for her to overcome her early fears and loneliness and to make the place her own. From the passion in her voice and the tears she was fighting back, it was clear how much she had invested in her case.

My friends were, at first, quite surprised at themselves, that they could have been so closed-minded. They realized that they would have made a terrible mistake if they had arbitrarily decided to send their younger daughter to that camp, if they hadn't really listened to their other daughter.

She was right, they decided, and so did their younger daughter. She could understand what her sister was saying. Fine, she said, she'd find another camp of her own. Looking at brochures and videotapes, she was able to make her selection within a couple of months. Her camp is on the other side of Maine, and a bit different in philosophy from the first, but it was her choice. My friends talked with her about the camp, listened closely, and could accept her choice.

These parents had listened with respect to their daughters, opened their own minds, and changed them. Imagine the positive effect of that, especially on their older daughter; imagine the lift to her self-esteem. Imagine, also, the positive effect on the relationship between the parents and their daughters.

It becomes critical in adolescence that your children have the feeling that you, too, will listen to them carefully, that they can trust you to think about what they have to say, that you might have a true disagreement with them without getting angry with them. Without that feeling, they simply won't have the necessary trust to turn to you with the serious issues of adolescence.

Now, during latency, you have countless opportunities for developing this new communication with respect. Many of these involve the first negotiations of independence.

Your daughter announces, for example, that she is the only person in her class who has to go to bed at 9:00. Isn't it time for her to be allowed to stay up until 10:00? A compromise of 9:30

would call for some give-and-take between the two of you. Or your son asks to be allowed to walk the two blocks to the video rental store by himself and to select his own Saturday night movie. Or to be allowed to take himself to school and back.

These requests are typical of the evolving, increasing responsibilities your child is reaching for. Your careful and respectful responses will allow him not only to start growing up but to feel that you really listen to him and that he can negotiate with you. These are terribly important feelings to carry into adolescence.

LAST CHANCE FOR LIMITS

The time for bed, the total hours of TV viewing, the amount of allowance, the use of the phone—these are all examples of privileges that establish lines of authority and structure, which become critical during adolescence.

Without that kind of parental structure, chaos often follows in adolescence. The child is accustomed to setting his own hours, his own rules. There is little to be negotiated. There are few limits on his life.

Being able to "ground" an adolescent, dock his allowance, or deny him a party, for example, because he has not been doing his homework is part of the shaping of adolescence. It doesn't work, however, if there is no pattern of discipline, of increasing rewards and responsibility.

I hope that you, as a parent, begin to set limits and establish structure in your child's earliest years, a point I make in our earlier book, *The Inner Child.* But if you do not, latency offers a second chance. As noted, this is a time when your child wants very much to please. That will make it easier for you to establish the rules of life and discipline that will benefit the two of you in the coming years.

PARENTS AS MODELS

The child's desire to please during this time comes into play in the phenomenon of modeling.

Children are now becoming finely tuned to the habits and styles of their parents. Increasingly, in conscious and unconscious ways—even while they are tentatively feeling out a new, separate identity of their own—they are identifying with their parents and trying to model themselves on them.

While this presents an opportunity for the development of healthy habits and attitudes, the opposite is also true. For example, I often hear parents moan about the hours and hours their children waste staring mindlessly at television. Not uncommonly, an accompanying concern is that the children have reading difficulties.

But the parents miss the connection between their children and themselves. If the parents watch TV from the time they arrive home from work until the time they go to bed, they are showing their children what seems to be an acceptable approach to TV viewing.

Not surprisingly in such a home, there are hardly any books around, even fewer being read by the parents. Without a word, then, the parents are conveying a message to their children about the importance of reading in their own lives.

Similarly, there are many reasons children start to smoke. It can relate to a need to impress their friends, for example. But the chances of becoming a smoker are infinitely greater if the parents light up. Here, too, an acceptable example is being presented to the child, intentionally or not. After all, what credibility does a smoking parent have when arguing with a child against smoking? "Don't make the mistake I did" is not strong enough.

Religion can also be affected by parental modeling. If the parents are asking their children to do as they say, not as they do, they will find themselves losing the argument. To the children, the real meaning of the importance of religious training—a boring interruption in their lives—is to be found in the fact that their parents do not go to church or synagogue, or pay much attention to religious observance.

So if getting your child confirmed or Bar Mitzvahed does have some importance for you, you are going to have to make a personal effort to demonstrate that. You are going to have to return to church and synagogue services.

The same holds for matters like overeating, smoking, and drinking. You are very much the model in the latency years. And it is worth noting that while parental modeling is meaningful to a child in other years, its impact is normally greatest during latency.

One other point on modeling and the attitude of "do as I say, not as I do." You could suffer doubly on such issues with that attitude. First, because your children won't buy it. They might still be young enough between seven and ten so that you can prevail and force your will on them. But they will quietly recognize the hypocrisy of your position. And second, that hypocrisy can haunt you later, in their adolescence. Certainly your credibility on these specific issues will be undermined. But further, your general authority will be endangered.

For adolescent encounters, you are drawing on trust and confidence and goodwill. It is such qualities that will allow your child to respond to you with some openness, some willingness to listen, to compromise. If there is a lingering cloud of hypocrisy hovering over you, filtering through your words, your whole position as a parent can be unconsciously eroded.

SAME-SEX ATTACHMENTS

For both girls and boys, the latency years are marked by sexual attachments to friends of the same sex. Girls relate to girls and boys relate to boys, which is technically homosexuality. But it is homosexuality of an unconscious sort and does not indicate any predisposition to committed homosexuality as a sexual identity.

I have found that parents have a certain amount of confusion over this phenomenon, and some alarm at the sexual play and explorations of their children. But it is all a natural stage of development.

In our society, girls of nine, ten, and eleven are allowed to be somewhat more sexual in their behaviors with one another than boys are. So we see them holding hands, hugging, kissing. Boys avoid such behavior, though in many other cultures men kiss and embrace in public in socially acceptable ways. Most boys in the United States learn that such behavior is not manly, and that means not even kissing your own father on the cheek.

One of the rituals of puberty for girls is the pajama party, an occasion of unconscious homosexuality. It is also a time for unconscious comparing of newly developing physical attributes. The pillow fights that occur during sleepovers have a homosexual component and reflect a most natural pubertal sex play.

Boys pass through this phenomenon a year or two later than girls, and while they don't normally go in for pajama parties, they manifest their homosexuality around this age with lots of wrestling and horsing around in locker rooms.

For boys, a kind of aggressive play is pervasive during this period and is encouraged by the actions of many of their sports heroes. Football and hockey are aggressive, brutal sports in which the toughest and the meanest are lionized. But even in other sports like baseball and basketball, strength and manliness are prized virtues. Their comic book and movie heroes wipe out entire armies with their superhuman strength.

Quite commonly at this time, boys also begin to explore their sexuality with each other, playing with each other's penises and mutually masturbating. Not surprisingly, when parents come upon such a scene, they are alarmed. But what is happening is part of a natural evolution.

In my experience, such sexual play indicates nothing more than typical development until about the age of fourteen. All the male and female homosexual patients I've worked with have reported that at least by age fourteen they knew their true sexual direction. While this observation is not the same as a conclusion based on a wide study, it does not contradict anything I've read.

During latency, girls and boys also pick up on cultural signals about their sexuality. For girls, this includes many of the superficial aspects of what their society expects of a woman: what clothes to wear, what manners to show, hairstyles, jewelry, even some aspects of behavior. It is okay, for example, for a girl to cry, to express emotional feelings quite openly. Boys, on the other hand, encounter a prohibition against such open emotionality, though this might be diminishing. They sense that aggressiveness is largely acceptable. They are allowed to be more phallic, if you will, in their play, their style, the way they look and act.

CHANGING SEXUALITY

There are, then, early stirrings of sexuality for both sexes, but these stirrings are still a giant step away from the surging awareness of adolescence. In a rather consistent way, latency is a period of modesty in general.

We see this first in the choice of cultural heroes. Michael Jackson was a fine example. Basically, to the ten-year-old, he was nonaggressive, semisexless (or at least he was before he was accused of sexual behavior with a young boy). Talent aside, there was nothing overt or threatening about his sexuality. He was even made up in a childish style.

Contrast that with, say, Madonna, whose public, performing persona revolves around flagrant sexuality. A friend of mine told me about the response of his eleven-year-old daughter to a Madonna concert on TV. The daughter is quite sophisticated in many ways, but after five minutes of watching Madonna prance around half-naked in a baldly suggestive routine, the girl got up and headed for the door, calling her "that slut" on the way out.

Nakedness is embarrassing to latency-age children. They demonstrate this attitude by asking their parents to give them some privacy; they want to undress alone, take a bath without supervision. They become especially sensitive to a parent of the opposite sex checking them out.

In this fragile environment, the first bra becomes a matter of some delicacy for young girls. Often, there is hardly enough breast development to require a bra, but for the girl, the issue is that of self-esteem. She's feeling good about herself and in a modest way wants to acknowledge that she's growing up.

In addition, she will probably show a great interest in cosmetics and in dressing as women do. How old should a child be to wear eye shadow? The answer is one for you to work out with your daughter. Are her eleven-year-old friends all wearing it?

Does your son feel he's ready for an earring? Are his friends all into earrings? With issues like eye shadow or earrings, you might want to give in to that kind of peer pressure, perhaps using this opportunity to practice a little negotiation.

Sex education during this transitional period will be somewhat dictated by the sexual growth of your child and somewhat reflective of the culture around you. Obviously, the early signs of puberty, which your child will be highly aware of insofar as they affect both the child personally and the people in the child's life, will lead to important questions. The girl will start wondering, what does this hair starting to grow down there mean? How big are my breasts going to get? What is menstruation, and when will it happen to me? The boy will have questions about erections, ejaculations, and wet dreams.

In my practice, I have found that many parents are uncomfortable talking much with their children about sexual matters, even at this elementary level. By the fourth grade, your child's school should be teaching the basic facts of bodies and sex, but that doesn't mean you should avoid the subject. Consider getting one or more of the many books that can help both children and parents. *What's Happening to My Body?* by Linda Madaras has a boys' edition and a girls' edition and does a nice job with fundamentals. *Growing Up* by Joanna Cole provides an introduction to the basics for both sexes. *Love and Sex and Growing Up* and *Love and Sex in Plain Language,* both by Eric W. Johnson, are also useful. You and your child can read sections separately or together, whichever you're comfortable with, and talk. Take it slowly, small sections at a time. At this age, children will get bored if you give them too much at once.

Your child will probably also have questions about AIDS, questions brought home from school or that result from watching the evening news on TV. The subject, like the disease itself, surrounds us.

Your discussion of AIDS can be incorporated with your talks about sex. You will want to provide the basic facts for your child: AIDS is a disease that is spread from one person to another, a very serious illness, and people get it by being physically intimate or by exchanging blood or bodily fluids. Children cannot get AIDS by kissing or hugging or having normal physical contact with someone. There has to be a clear exchange of blood or bodily fluids.

This discussion may or may not lead to questions about intercourse, a subject so many parents find extremely uncomfortable discussing with their children. But at this level, the discussion will likely be quite limited. "That is what a grown man and a woman do together. It's how they make babies. If one of them has AIDS, he or she can give it to the other."

Your child might also ask about AIDS and homosexuals. While it will be important in early adolescence for your child to start understanding that there are people attracted to people of the same sex and what this means, a detailed explanation is probably more than your preadolescent can grasp. A simple statement to the effect that in the United States, AIDS first spread widely among homosexual men—men who are attracted to other men and not to women—will probably suffice.

Of course, any talk of AIDS provides an opportunity to warn about drugs. You might already have made the point with your child that drugs are poison, but now you can point out that drug addicts generally share drug needles and that in New York, for example, the sharing of needles is the primary transmitter of AIDS.

SCHOOLS AND ACCOMPLISHMENTS: WHOSE AMBITIONS?

During the latency years, many parents make important decisions about the schools their children will attend. The whole universe of schools changes.

As a child begins to emerge from the lower school grades, the learning process becomes increasingly demanding. Math moves beyond simple addition and subtraction. Essays that call upon some powers of abstraction and analysis are a regular part of homework. The applications of language on paper and in speech unfold in startling forms.

With these developments, you begin to get a clearer picture of your child as a student. It is not simply that he seems attentive and relates well with other children, as you were told by his teachers in grades two and three. Now they are talking to you about how well he grasps multiplication tables and whether he is able to write a book review that does more than present the obvious facts about a book.

As the picture sharpens, you may have to reconsider the ideas you had about him as a student and rethink your choice of schools. In the midst of this process, you may very well unconsciously project many of your personal ambitions and fantasies onto your child.

Anna Freud touched on this tendency in her book *Normality and Pathology in Childhood:* "There are parents whose attachment to the child depends on the latter's representing for them either an ideal of themselves or a figure of their own past. . . . Some mothers, or fathers, assign to the child a role in their own pathology and relate to the child on this basis, not on the basis of the child's real needs."*

So perhaps your choice of school for your child reflects your unconscious needs for yourself, rather than the educational needs of your child.

This can happen quite subtly. I think of a couple in suburban Boston who placed their sons in a school that appealed to them— both overachievers—as a place that was unpretentious, conservative, demanding. As they later realized, they both had needs to succeed in such academically rigorous environments. But the school was a disaster for their children.

This didn't become obvious until their older son reached the fifth grade; as the work became substantially more difficult, he had increasing problems. The school was not supportive. Basically, the staff told the parents that if the boy was having difficulty, he should get a tutor.

At first, the parents went along with this suggestion, but when they saw that no matter how hard their son worked, he still was not making much progress, they knew they needed other answers. Though the boy was having difficulties, he was not stupid. Not surprisingly, he was becoming depressed.

They pushed the school for answers, or at least helpful obser-

Normality and Pathology in Childhood: Assessments of Development by Anna Freud. Madison, Conn.: International Universities Press, Inc., 1965, p. 47.

vations. But they got none. Finally, after several meetings with teachers, and conversations with other parents having similar problems—half the boy's class turned out to be working with tutors—they woke up.

They realized that this was a school that cared very little about its students. Either a child could handle its curriculum, or the child, not the school, had a problem. Both these parents were psychologically minded and had had psychotherapy. As they explored possible solutions, they also considered how they had made such a mistake in the first place. They realized that their own unconscious ambitions for their boys to excel academically and to rise to some mighty Ivy League school had blinded them.

With this new insight, they conducted an anxious search for a new school. Fortunately, the greater Boston area offers a variety of choices, and they were able to find a very different school. At this institution, the student was placed at the heart of the educational process, and a student's problem with any subject was one that the school accepted as its own and worked with the student to overcome. This warm and supportive place also had a reasonably demanding curriculum, but it was a much less competitive school. Its students ended up in perfectly good colleges, including some in the Ivy League, although that seemed the farthest goal from the school's objectives.

In every meaningful way, this school was light-years apart from the first place. The parents transferred their children, and both boys flourished.

I am frequently reminded of their experience when I encounter other parents who are blind to their own unconscious needs, pushing their children into schools that are completely unsuited for them.

And not only into schools. The same blindness leads parents to push their defenseless children into all kinds of inappropriate lessons and activities: to try to make Olympic swimmers and gymnasts of them, or professional football players of them, for example. The tennis courts of America are littered with the shells of young adolescents who were manipulated and twisted by their hopelessly driven parents who, quite unaware of their own needs, pushed their children far beyond healthy competition, far beyond the point where the adolescents wanted to go or were capable of going.

These are all, of course, variations on the most famous model of such a parent, the stage mother or father. Later in this chapter, I speak of the damage that can be inflicted on a child who is forced into the narrow life of the theater, or dance, or music, to the exclusion of other pursuits, and the sad consequences when that great effort does not quite succeed, which is usually the case.

The price of such parental blindness can be terribly high. I treated one boy who responded to the severe pressure of his parents—they stuck him in a horrendously competitive school he could not handle—by developing ulcerative colitis. He was trying to accommodate his parents in order to retain their love, and in the process he was bleeding badly.

His parents were both extremely intelligent and accomplished, very driven professionals, but I couldn't get them to understand that what their son needed was not six hours of homework every night but a good night's sleep because he was bleeding and anemic. They were incapable of accepting that, or my suggestion that they consider some other school for him.

Still, I was allowed to work with the boy, and over the years, through psychotherapy and medication, he became more relaxed and physically stronger. He also survived the punishing school and graduated, always maintaining that anything less would have been too devastating for his parents. Only when the ordeal was over could he see that what he had suffered could have and should have been avoided, and that he and his parents might have worked out a different solution.

Out of such experiences, I offer parents a caution: when you are making such a critical decision for your child's life as choosing a school, examine your own needs. How much of the decision reflects your own inner desires and fantasies, and how much of it truly suits your child's needs?

In the cases described above, mistakes were made, but not because the parents were indifferent or uncaring. I have encountered a number of other cases, however, in which the choice of school was basically a way for the parents to reject their child: they sent him off to boarding school.

I do not mean to suggest that every child sent to boarding school is unwanted. Not at all. Frequently, boarding school is a family tradition, and not to send the child represents a form of rejection.

But consider the case of the upper-class couple who came to me with their eleven-year-old son. The boy had a learning disability and after years of being rejected by his parents was deeply depressed. He had just flunked out of one prep school. His father had decided that the boy's problem was that he was lazy. What he needed, the man announced, was a good military school to shape him up. His wife seemed to agree.

It was clear from talking with them that they had invested great emotional hopes and dreams in this boy, and that they were sorely disappointed. It was also clear that the boy felt unloved, unwanted, and generally worthless.

A military academy should be the last place in the world to send such a child. And I tried to explain to the parents that there were prep schools that offered special training that could help the boy with his learning problem. I told them he also needed psychotherapy.

I don't think I made much of a dent. They were rigid people and had their minds made up. I don't know what happened to that sad young boy.

These days I hear a certain amount of rationalizing in the argument for boarding schools: that sending children off to these places removes them from the dangers of drugs and sex that adolescents face at home.

But this is a myth.

In the course of treating many boarding school students, I've found that these schools are subject to the same social problems as the rest of our society.

Drugs are available. Usually, one of the students with psychopathic problems becomes the dealer on campus after being contacted by outside sources. Professional drug dealers have long recognized that within these enclaves there is a market of relatively wealthy children. As for sex, the children are quite sexually active, especially as they approach fifteen and sixteen years of age. After all, there is not nearly as much adult supervision in a boarding school as in a home.

I certainly do not mean to condemn boarding schools. But I think it is important for any parents choosing one for their child to examine their reasons. Is it a successful family tradition? Fine. Given the choice of local schools, is it the best educational alternative for the child? Fine. Parents should try to take care that they're not using these schools to hide their own failures.

SPECIAL TALENTS

During these latency years, children with special talents begin to reveal them. What was a flair for acting and the excitement of a couple of school plays blossoms into something more. The interest deepens; the talent flourishes. Or perhaps it's ballet, or the piano, or ice skating, or some other sport in which the child has shown early signs of promise and now raises skills to a more advanced level.

For parents, such a development presents some difficult questions. How much do you want not only to encourage but to push such talents? If you exclude other activities and options from the child's life, what is the price the child pays? Is it worth it?

Here again, you must look very closely at your motives: whose dreams are you chasing, yours or the child's?

My advice is to move slowly.

One of the best examples I have seen is a mother who responded to her stagestruck daughter, but she did not allow the child to push her, nor did she push the child. The child was talented and landed roles in two Broadway shows. But the course was a modulated one. Nobody rushed to sign up an agent the moment the child voiced her passions. (Indeed, passions at this age can be fleeting, perhaps attached to a passing identification with a cultural hero: That man or woman is a movie star, so I want to be one too.) There was no agent allowed in the picture to rush life, nor was her life reshaped around her success. These parents did not want to eliminate normalcy from their daughter's life or to take away her normal options.

The fact is that real success in any of the areas we're discussing is extremely rare. What happens if everything is risked on becoming a prima ballerina, and the bubble bursts? Perhaps after years of narrow dedication, the girl turns out to be not quite good enough? Or she breaks an ankle? The failure that results is not just a sad career crash. There is also the feeling of being a personal failure that haunts such people.

The broader a child's base, the more diversity in her personality, the more options she has in life. In our culture, completing high school allows you to expand your job choices. Completing college increases those possibilities many times over and broadens your life. This is what I point out to adolescents who are thinking about dropping out of high school or college. It's good advice for them. And it's something to think about for the parent of a child with special talents.

In my view, you can encourage such gifts and interests,

you can make the road a little smoother, but you don't have to push.

When you allow your child to pursue a special interest, it shouldn't be at the expense of other interests.

Let's take music as an example. I spoke in the previous chapter of how your latency child may show early signs of independence by choosing music that's different from yours. Commonly, this is more than a superficial connection; the child dives into that music, becoming as knowledgeable about his favorite groups as you are about your favorite string quartet. Such an interest often leads to a desire to experiment, to feel life out. The guitar is neat, he thinks, why not try the guitar? And, of course, the guitar is much cooler than the piano, toward which you have been steering him.

This situation offers you the precious opportunity to follow his lead, rather than imposing your interests on him. When you can do that, the results can be impressive. His personal investment in the choice will be that much greater, and most likely so will his effort to succeed at it. And success in *some* personal effort, as we'll see, is critically important at this age.

So you follow his lead, let him try the guitar; he likes it and shows some talent for it. For him, an issue of independence becomes a source of self-esteem. By all means, encourage him. Yet at the same time allow everything else in his life to develop as before. He still plays basketball and tennis with a passion. He still does his homework with reasonable results in school. He still tries out for a part in the class play.

The guitar playing continues, and before long he has enough confidence to form a band. They start to play at parties, and by the time he is in high school, he and the group have some real notoriety around the school.

Not only does this success further his self-esteem, it increases his sexual feelings about himself. The lead guitarist in a rock-and-roll band is often something of a sex symbol, and some of that rubs off on him. He dates more easily and finds himself more confident on these dates.

The guitar and his interest in music may or may not continue after high school. Perhaps he'll want to major in music in college or go to a place like Julliard. Or maybe other interests will become more important to him, so he plays the guitar only for his own pleasure, occasionally to entertain friends.

What matters is that he has options. He did not reshape his life, bending it around his passion for the guitar. We all know people like the acquaintance of mine who became a lawyer but never really abandoned his passion for the piano; now, at age sixty, he is about to retire from the law to pursue a career as a club and studio pianist.

A child should come out of latency with a positive sense of self, with a sense that she is good at something. It might come from athletics, or scholastic achievements, or from being good enough with a guitar to play in a band in front of a room full of peers. It doesn't really matter *where* that feeling of accomplishment comes from, so long as it enables the child to feel good about herself. Otherwise, the child enters adolescence with serious self-esteem problems.

A parent can nurture this development through positive re-inforcement, by remembering how important it is for children to hear compliments as well as criticism from their parents.

Through the early years, when parents are often greatly concerned with setting limits on their children and teaching them, the balance of life can easily become negative. Nearly everything coming from the parent is a restriction, a correction. "No, no, no, no. Let Mommy show you how." Depending on a parent's own problems, well-intended guidance can become excessive. Then the child is continually undermined, and self-esteem is shattered.

It's a good rule, especially in latency, to balance anything negative you say to your child with something positive. Don't fake it; children have keen detectors for the phony. You need not make the positive statement immediately after the critical remark. But at some point during that day, balance the ledger.

Children will respond to positive input as well as negative, and they need to have a sense that their parents appreciate them, like them, think well of them.

3

Sex and Sexuality:
The Classical Battlefield
with No Safe Towers

For the parent of an adolescent, there is probably no area more complicated and explosive than the sexual.

Up to now, the whole matter of sex might have been uncomfortable, perhaps embarrassing. Explaining sexual mechanics to a child is not easy for most parents. Questions from children about what Mommy and Daddy do in bed are sticky. Dealing sensitively with a child's sexual explorations of her own body can be somewhat unnerving. But all of that is child's play, if you will, compared with the sexual specter of the adolescent years.

Now the child-becoming-young-adult is capable of not merely fantasizing but acting.

Parents have countless fears, from the traditional ones of accidental pregnancy and venereal disease to the current one of AIDS. They also have nonmedical concerns: How to protect their child from the painful emotional experiences of sex coming too soon, before the child feels ready for it. How to find a way to allow their children to enjoy physical intimacy without being intimidated by it. How to help him develop his own persona in relation to someone of the other sex.

There is an unconscious response as well, the unexpected feelings over the new sexuality of a son or daughter. For parents who are uneasy with their own sexuality, a child's development can be threatening, upsetting. It can be extremely difficult for such parents to respond to their child in reasonable ways. (What is really going on when a mother calls me in alarm because her eighteen-year-old daughter wants desperately to go off for a skiing weekend with three girlfriends and four boys?)

Out of fear, confusion, a feeling of being personally threatened, parents often make the sexual area a massive struggle for control.

But short of locking children away in the tower, there is no absolute control that parents can have. There are other powerful ways parents can influence their children, which we'll consider. But first, stop and think about this: sex is ubiquitous in our society.

TIMES HAVE CHANGED

In terms of sexual acceptance and activity, our culture has changed radically since I was growing up in the 1940s and 1950s. And the changes require a new awareness on the part of parents in educating their children. It is not easy to come by.

Put simply, in my youth, there was a real danger in having intercourse with a young woman, and it wasn't AIDS. It was getting stuck in a shotgun marriage. Abortion was rare, mostly illegal. Condoms were unpleasant and undependable, diaphragms didn't work very well, and there was no pill. The so-called sex manuals that were supposed to teach adolescents about sex were ridiculously circumspect with their discussions of chickens and eggs and their stick-figure drawings. Most of the girls I knew learned about such matters from a booklet that came with their Tampax. While attending Harvard in the 1950s, I was astonished, and so was everyone I knew there, when *Playboy* appeared with bare-breasted women.

Contrast that era with what surrounds us today. Sex in limitless flavors is available to your child in the magazines at the corner newsstand. R-rated movies show nudity and quite explicit sexual situations. On standard TV, characters might still keep their clothes on, but their actions and language are pervasively sexual. On popular call-in radio shows, people discuss their sexual questions and problems with a vividness that can be stunning.

According to studies I've read, at the time I was in high school, fewer than 10 percent of the women were sexually active, whereas today the average age for the first sexual intercourse for girls is 16.2 years of age, for boys, 15.7. By the age of 20, 77 percent of females and 86 percent of males are sexually active. A 1989 survey showed that more than one million teenage girls become pregnant in the United States every year—one out of every ten girls under the age of 20.

People frequently ask me if the impact of the media in this area is good or bad, but I don't think that is the point. What matters is how this material is digested and dealt with by the family.

As a result of the changes in sexual mores, there is a genuine need for children to become sophisticated about sexuality at an early age. Certainly, open discussions about body parts and how babies are conceived should begin somewhere between the ages of nine and ten. By the time children are twelve to thirteen, they should not only understand the mechanics of the sexual act but begin to comprehend the ideas of intimacy and love that are, one hopes, a part of it. And by this age, they should be aware that there are people of the same sex who have intimate relationships. Today they should also understand the risks involved in unprotected sex, most especially that of AIDS. And though AIDS has overshadowed venereal diseases, they should know that sexual promiscuity can lead to many serious venereal diseases.

PARENTS AS SEX EXPERTS

When parents are uncomfortable teaching their children about sex, it will show. The parent, then the child, will grow embarrassed, and the child will be left feeling anxious, wondering what is so repellent and forbidden about this subject.

Parents can explore their own feelings around this issue, but they should also recognize that they do not have to be sex experts in order to be good parents.

Many schools, public and private, have sex education courses as part of their regular curriculum. Planned Parenthood offers books and pamphlets and discussion programs which I have found to be solid and trustworthy. You will want to examine these courses and publications for yourself, of course, and be sure you feel comfortable with what is being taught. Assuming that you are, you might do what countless parents do and use what the school, for example, is teaching as a point of departure for discussions with your own child. Many parents, in other words, find that when left to their own devices, instructing their children is too disturbing, but if they have material to refer to, they are able to talk about applying that material to life around them.

As I noted in the previous chapter, books can help get around the awkwardness about sex. Those suggested for latency-age children are also appropriate for early adolescents: *What's Happening to My Body?* by Linda Madaras, *Growing Up* by Joanna Cole, and Eric W. Johnson's *Love and Sex and Growing Up* and *Love and Sex in Plain Language*. For early adolescents, *You're in Charge: Teenage Girl's Guide to Sex and Her Body* by Niels Lawrenson is helpful, as are two that answer questions about homosexuality, *When Somebody You Know Is Gay* by Susan and David Cohen, and *Understanding Sexual Identity: A Book for Gay and Lesbian Teens and Their Friends* by Janice Reich.

If you want to use books as tools, don't simply pass them to your child. Each of you should read sections and then talk about the material.

Try not to avoid the issue altogether. It is central to your child's development at this time. If you do not even acknowledge it, you are pushing your child away and sending a confusing message. Remember, by adolescence, your child realizes that his parents are sexual creatures too. What will he think if they seem to deny their sexuality to him? In fact, one of the ways you can make contact on this loaded issue is to talk about your own experiences as an adolescent, your own difficulties coming to grips with what was then your new sexuality.

Frequently, adolescents feel most comfortable talking about sexual matters with a parent of the same sex. A thirteen-year-old boy can be assured by his father that "wet dreams" are natural, age-appropriate events, and a girl of that age is best guided through menses by her mother. (For a single parent, the best solution is to have a friend or relative of the opposite sex whom the child likes fill that role, if possible.)

There's a movie I recommend to parents of adolescents that gives them a glimpse into an adolescent fantasy: *Dirty Dancing.* Here is a girl, still known to her family as Baby, the summer before she goes off to college, struggling with her own independence and sexual identity. At a summer resort, attracted to a handsome dance instructor, she wrestles with all the basic questions: Should I? Shouldn't I? Will I? Won't I? What will be the effects of my behavior? Where are my parents in all this? If I do it, will I get pregnant? Will they stand by me?

ENDURING ATTITUDES

Some attitudes among adolescents are slow to change.

In the media, there has been a certain amount of speculation about a new sexuality among adolescents, a change that reflects the broader shifts in roles for women. Certainly, today's adolescents are growing up with new female models. Chances are, their mothers work. Educational and career opportunities for women have expanded enormously in a generation. Yet I don't hear that the exciting ambition among thirteen-year-old girls is to become a bank president. Nor do I yet see a comparable shift among adolescent girls in their perceived sexual roles.

Once again, in the popular media, there is talk of a new type of male, an adolescent who is gentler, more respectful of girls, less concerned with his macho image. But I don't see this change—at least not yet. The young men, for the most part, continue to identify with a cultural model of male assertiveness, of male dominance over female submission. And among female adolescents, I still notice preference for the macho guy. They like a somewhat aggressive, pushy male. They still go for the football hero. They still want the boy to decide which movie or restaurant they'll go to on their date.

It seems to me that the traditional double standard continues to exist. Parents still feel that it's acceptable for boys to gain sexual experience at seventeen or eighteen, whereas girls should remain virginal until they finally live with a man.

Feminists would argue, I think, that society has to change more, and that mothers have to start raising their children with new attitudes from birth. I would agree with them on both counts, and I believe we will eventually see this happen. But for now, while there is an abundance of sexual license in society in general and among adolescents in particular, there is a noticeable time lag in terms of the effect on adolescent sexual and cultural roles.

SEXUAL IDENTITY AND
HOMOSEXUALITY

One of the essential tasks of adolescence is to establish sexual identity, to reach a point where the teenager can say: I am a man or woman, and I feel relatively comfortable with that.

Freudians view adolescence as a time when the child works through the Oedipal complex again. The male abandons his unconscious sexual wishes for his mother, abandons the idea that he can replace his father in this manner, and allows himself to relate to other females. The female abandons her unconscious desires for her father, her competition with her mother for him, and allows herself to develop relations with other males.

In the process of adolescent discovery, a minority of teenagers—estimated at 10 percent—find themselves to be homosexual. Essentially, they arrive at their conclusions in the same ways and on the same developmental schedule as heterosexuals. By the time they are thirteen or fourteen, they have a fairly strong sense that they are homosexual, and somewhere around the age of sixteen, they are certain of it.

In my experience, dealing with a child's homosexuality is the most traumatic kind of family sexual problem.

I think of a young gay woman who had accepted her homosexuality in adolescence and kept it from her family. Attending college in New York, she started living with a woman, an arrangement her family took to be the usual sharing of an apartment. She saw no need to say anything to her parents, extremely traditional and older people, for she knew they would be devastated by the truth. But her parents kept matching her up with one young man after another, and she was being forced into a difficult position.

Finally, she came to me, shaken and unsure of how to proceed. I saw her twice, and we came to the conclusion that she had no choice. She had to tell her parents that she wasn't terribly interested in relationships with men. And that she didn't think she wanted to be married.

The next thing I knew, her father was on the phone to me, very upset, asking me to treat her and "straighten her out." I told him I could treat her, but he should understand that if his daughter was homosexual, therapy was not going to make that go away. No one really knew what caused homosexuality, I explained, or the relative importance of psychological as opposed to biological factors.

What he absorbed and accepted, I don't know. But I did treat his daughter for a while. She had problems in her life she was interested in working on, and we tackled them together. She was content with her sexuality and her lesbian relationship, and at one point I told her what I tried to tell her father: "I'm not going to try to change you."

Eventually, her relationship with her father pretty much worked itself out. She became self-supporting and was able to dictate new terms between them. I don't think her father was ever able to accept her homosexuality, but at least he made some effort to keep her in the family.

I had another case in which the father was so disturbed by the homosexuality of his sixteen-year-old son that he threw the boy out of their home. Seeing that his son was both homosexual and extremely effeminate, the father reacted as if his own masculinity were threatened. His attitude was that such a son simply could not come from his gene pool; his wife must have conceived this boy with someone else. Although this man had inherited quite a bit of money, he banished his son without a dollar. The boy lived from hand to mouth with relatives, his mother sneaking money to him.

The mother tried to reason with the man, but it was hopeless. They fought and later divorced. The boy set off on his own, ended up selling clothes in California. He contacted me, and at his wise request I put him in touch with a therapist who helped him gain perspective on the traumas of his earlier shattered life.

Frequently, parents of homosexuals come to me in tears and confusion. They speak about their changing their sons and daughters, but I tell them their children are not motivated to change. I try to explain to them that being gay is what we call "ego syntonic"—the ego is comfortable with the homosexuality, their sons and daughters are happy with themselves as they are. At times, I have used the analogy of losing weight. "How much do you want to lose weight?" I ask them. "Well, I try, and I do," they respond. "Yes, you try, but there's a part of you that really does not want to change, that wants to stay as you are." They agree with that. "Well, you have to understand that the whole of your son (or daughter) at the moment wants to stay the way he is. That being the case, what do you think I'm going to be able to do, even if I can get him in this office?"

If they can accept that idea, they can give up some of the fantasy that I can change their son or daughter, and then we can talk more coherently. As a result, they are soon able to say to their child, "Okay, we know you're not going to change. But could you go see Dr. Gabriel once or twice, so that he can help us understand what's going on, and we can talk to each other again?"

Often the children have used their announcement as a hostile weapon. Indeed, in the 1980s, there seemed to be a wave of "coming out" declarations shouted from the barricades. Although that appears to have passed, I still find hostility on a quieter level. And if the adolescent comes in a couple of times, I do try to get the idea across to her, "Why can't you go a little easier on your parents? Why do you have to bash them over the head?"

I have never seen a case where a child's homosexuality was not a tremendous shock to a family. But not all families with gay children end up in psychiatrists' offices. I hear of parents who are able to absorb the shock, to discuss the meaning of this sexuality with their child, and often, with the help of support groups for parents of gays, to come to terms with such a troubling and puzzling development in their child. And, most important, these parents are able to sustain loving relationships in the family.

NEW CULTURAL HEROES

Children's evolving sexuality during adolescence is reflected in their choice of new cultural heroes. In latency, children wanted to be like their favorite performers, to be able to sing and dance like them. There was a rather simple identification with figures of the same sex. Then the attraction shifted to androgynous stars. Michael Jackson, as I noted in the previous chapter, appealed to children between the ages of ten and twelve. His shirt was open and he danced wildly, but his sexuality was not overwhelming or threatening to the young viewer. By thirteen, the adolescent girl has abandoned Jackson, as if he were a transitional object, like a "blankie" from infancy. She is ready for Axl Rose and overt sexuality.

In the preceding chapter, I mentioned the eleven-year-old girl who walked out of the room after watching five minutes of Madonna prancing about in a TV concert, muttering "That slut," as she left. In fact, three years later, at age fourteen, she was committed to Guns N' Roses.

INPUT FROM PEERS VERSUS PARENTS

The choice of favorite music, TV, film stars is, of course, much affected by peers. So are attitudes toward sex.

Somewhere between ages twelve and thirteen, much of the talk among your daughter and her friends focuses on sex and their ideas and misconceptions of what goes on. It's amazing how misinformation passes from one generation to another, and then from one teenager to another. The idea, for example, that a girl can't get pregnant if the boy removes his penis in time. Or that intercourse just before or during or just after a period is completely safe.

Peers can also pressure an adolescent to become sexually active, certainly by the ages of fifteen and sixteen. For many children, being an accepted member of their own group is tremendously important, even if it means violating the social standards of their parents.

Peter Blos, the Freudian theoretician on adolescence, speaks about "uniformism," in which the teenager accepts a code of behavior in a way that permits her to divorce her own feelings from her actions. Her motivation, in other words, is to be equal in outward behavior to others, to live up to group norms. And it all happens unconsciously. The young woman does not inwardly debate right and wrong, what you, her parents, have told her as opposed to what her friends are urging on her. She does not even consult her own feelings.

This new attitude frequently leads to a fundamental struggle between you and your child.

Must you lock your daughter up in the tower? Or can you talk to her?

Let's assume you have a reservoir of goodwill that has been filled over the years. I don't think it's very effective to draw on that goodwill by suggesting, "If you love us, you won't have sex until you're married." Unless you live in an extremely isolated part of America, those days are over.

What you say at the critical ages—fourteen, fifteen, sixteen—is probably going to be the most persuasive if you speak from the heart and provide sound information.

You also need to listen to and empathize with your daughter, but don't expect her to come to you and say, "I'm thinking about having sex this weekend. What do you think?" The communication, I assure you, is more complicated than that.

If the two of you have a trusting relationship, you will be able to talk intimately, and she will probably surprise you with her openness. In those private times just before she goes off to sleep, she will chat about school and her friends—how Alice has nothing on her mind but boys, and Mary has become a slut. When she speaks this way, she is reaching out to you, and you can talk to her at these times about what matters most to you. About your hopes that she can understand the importance of having intimacy and closeness before sex. About the way anyone can be overwhelmed by the pressures of a group. About how the need to look cool, to be accepted by a group can lead a person to become promiscuous, even though she may not be emotionally ready for sex, even though she may not even enjoy the act itself.

You will also want to provide her with information about venereal disease and AIDS, so she can make intelligent independent judgments. Every year, 2.5 million adolescents are infected with sexually transmitted diseases, including a lot of syphilis, gonorrhea, and herpes among middle- and upper-middle-class kids. A warning in itself will not be very effective, but if you put it in a sympathetic context, the message sounds quite different. For example, "I'm not trying to stop you from loving somebody and caring for them and being involved with them, but you do have to be very careful since diseases can be communicated when people are intimate and have sex."

Getting this point across is not easy. Frequently, you will encounter the profound sense of denial that affects so many adolescents, the sense of omnipotence. "Someone else might catch syphilis, not me." This omnipotence appears to be the psychological counterpart of the adolescent's newly discovered physical growth and power. It affects his judgment. A real sexual risk might be ignored.

Earlier, I noted that by adolescence parents can no longer prevail by edict. Sex is a vivid example. Not that you should be silent. You should be continually letting your child know what you think and feel and why. "Look, I'm not fool enough to think that you won't be tempted to sleep with somebody, especially if you get close to them. But I have to tell you that I don't approve of that when you are fifteen, and I don't think it's very wise." This is all part of communication and negotiation, which are at the heart of the adolescent period.

Also important at this time is deciding when to transfer authority to your child for taking care of her own life. The dilemma of the mother on the phone I mentioned at the beginning of this chapter serves as a good example. Should she allow her daughter to go on the ski trip, where four girls and four boys, all eighteen and nineteen years old, all seniors in high school, would have no adult supervision?

I sympathized with her plight. It seemed to me that she and her husband could simply sit down with their daughter and say, "Look, this trip frightens us." They could be completely open about their fears.

They might also decide that their days of controlling such actions were over. After all, in a matter of months their daughter would be off at college, living a life of her own away from home. If she wanted to go on such a ski weekend then, she might or might not tell her parents before going, but there would be no issue of permission and control. So her parents might acknowledge all of this and say, "We don't think this is a good idea, but it's up to you."

Or if they were still sufficiently worried, they could explain their concerns and say that once she was on her own at college, they would not try to interfere in such matters. But while she was still living at home, they felt they had to be honest with her— and themselves—and say no.

I did not share with the woman one more thought that crossed my mind. If her child was going to act out sexually, she would find a place to do it. I think this is a general rule for adolescents from about the age of sixteen.

If two adolescents are involved in a passionate relationship and they want to have sex, there is little a parent can rely on, except the sense of trust and the messages that have been communicated earlier. The parent now hopes that these feelings and ideas have become enmeshed in the very fabric of the adolescent's days and nights, growth and judgment.

4

Drugs and Alcohol:
The Need for Calm
Confrontation

Along with sex, the foremost concerns of parents of adolescents these days are drugs and alcohol. The three areas have a number of similarities, including the developmental issues that are involved, the adolescent's attitudes and behavior, and the parent's way of coping.

Just as we saw with sex, educating a child about drugs and alcohol will have a profound effect on his attitudes. And the best time to do this teaching is during the latency stage, when the child is between the ages of seven and ten.

PARENTS AS ROLE MODELS

Your habits and behavior will teach the first lessons. If you and/or your spouse are smokers, your child will assume that smoking is acceptable. On the other hand, if you have given up smoking, as increasing numbers of adults are doing, that message should be delivered quite clearly. "Yes, I used to smoke, at least a pack a day. But I gave it up years ago, when I learned that smoking kills you. Now I can't even stand the smell of tobacco."

Maybe your obstetrician told you when you became pregnant that he wouldn't treat you through pregnancy or deliver your baby unless you stopped smoking immediately, so damaging can smoking be for a fetus. And so you stopped. That's a powerful story for a young person to hear: Not only did Mommy give up smoking, just like that, but she did it for me.

The way you treat alcohol in your home teaches another lesson. Heavy drinking on your part condones heavy drinking in general. Take the parent who comes home from work and immediately reaches for a drink, then sighs with relief as the first flush of alcohol hits his system, maybe even declaring: "Boy, I needed that." That parent is encouraging his child to do the same when the child grows up a bit.

The above example might seem a bit overdrawn, but stop and look at your own habits. In a culture where alcohol is widely blended into the fabric of everyday living, where it is part of business meetings and entertaining, where heavy drinking is the rule at social gatherings, a pattern—more addictive than most people realize—is established and accepted. In fact, many people who use alcohol in their lives are probably much more dependent on it than they realize or would care to admit. Undoubtedly, they are not aware of the model they are presenting to their children.

At the same time, alcohol, unlike drugs, is a legal substance in our society. And for many people, alcohol used in a limited manner is a socially accepted part of their lives. I think especially of drinking wine or beer. Certainly, they can also be abused, but when approached as an accompaniment to food, as a way of enhancing a meal, their place in life is quite different.

Parents who drink wine moderately with their dinner might do well to educate their children to that use of wine, first by example and then as the children grow older, by letting them taste the wine and learn about it. Wines are interesting in their characteristics, in the differences between one wine and another, differences in grapes and vintages. Without turning family meals into seminars, you can pass along wine information in an easy manner when a particular wine is being tasted.

Beyond the wine knowledge, the child picks up an approach to wine and to drinking in general that should help shape her attitude toward drinking in later years. Specifically, that there is a measured, reasonable approach to drinking that is acceptable and pleasurable.

There are parents, of course, who want their children to be teetotalers, and obviously, such parents should try to convince their children not to try the stuff. I am skeptical, however. Alcohol is so ubiquitous in our society, I don't think that approach will work, unless it comes out of a religious background and an accepted religious commitment by the child and the family.

Parental modeling works the same for drugs as it does for alcohol. If you or your spouse smoke marijuana, for example, expect your children to do the same. If you use other drugs, in addition to the other problems you can count on, you will be showing your children what you consider acceptable.

THE POWERFUL FACTS

Educating your children about drugs and alcohol should be easier than educating them about sex. The complex emotions attached to sex, which usually makes discussions of sex so difficult for both parents and children, are not present here. Nevertheless, there might be some resistance on the part of the latency child, certainly from the young adolescent, resistance related to issues of independence.

Drugs and alcohol, after all, symbolize a new, adult status.

Parental warnings can easily be perceived by adolescents as efforts to block them from achieving their independence. Claiming that marijuana destroys brains, for example, can shatter a parent's credibility and feed the independence struggle. All the more reason to keep discussions factual. The facts, especially when delivered in a calm manner, are powerful in themselves.

Take marijuana, for example. It can affect the brain, the testes, and the ovaries, and it is biochemically toxic to the liver and other organs. The chemical tetrahydrocannaboid (THC) is the mood-altering element in marijuana, and once in the body it attaches to organs. In the brain, it causes hallucinations. In the sex organs, it can disrupt the menstrual cycle and result in temporary infertility. There is evidence that THC is a threat to the genetic fragmentation of chromosomes, that it affects the formation of DNA, the genetic material that controls the growth of cells. And one joint does as much damage to the lungs as a whole pack of cigarettes. Marijuana can induce panic and over the long term may seriously affect a user's mental health, contributing to anxiety, nurturing paranoia and psychosis. And, of course, marijuana is illegal.

Alcohol is absorbed directly into the bloodstream, quickly reaching the brain and impairing coordination. The smaller the person, the less alcohol required to upset stability. Alcohol also affects the brain by reducing inhibitions and building a false sense of power. Not surprisingly, then, one of the foremost causes of adolescent death is driving while drunk. And until one is eighteen (or twenty-one, or whatever the legal age for drinking is in your state), consuming alcohol is illegal. Alcohol can make you nauseous and sick, even knock you out. In the long term, it can make you fat, damage your liver, your brain, even kill you.

Both marijuana and alcohol remove normal controls on behavior, a point well worth making with a young adolescent. "Do you really want to be at a party, possibly with a number of people you don't know, and not have control over yourself, over what you say and do, over what is done to you?"

A number of drugs, like heroin, are usually injected, raising the possibility of AIDS infection astronomically. In fact, shared needles are the single largest cause of the spread of AIDS in New York today.

Two good sources for drug and alcohol information are the American Council for Drug Education (301-294-0600) and the National Clearinghouse for Alcohol and Drug Information (800-729-6686). The latter is a federally funded operation that distributes government studies, pamphlets, and the like.

The facts in themselves are powerful. If you can discuss drugs and alcohol with a straightforward approach, you can somewhat defuse the issue. You can remove it from the parent-child realm in which you are giving orders and/or threatening. Instead, you are presenting some rather serious and convincing evidence and asking your children to consider it and to act with it in mind.

This will help with power struggles that erupt so easily over drug and alcohol use. "I'll do what I want to do. . . . You can't tell me not to try liquor," the adolescent says, or at least thinks. The issue then becomes a symbol of control and independence. The facts become blurred or forgotten.

Even if a power struggle occurs, this is one issue where a strong relationship can prevail, where you can draw on the trust and love you have built over the years with your son or daughter. You can say clearly, "Look, I respect you and I know you are not a little kid. But I have to tell you again that drugs and alcohol are dangerous, which you know better than I, and I have to ask you again not to get started with them. Please." In my experience, this kind of clear but respectful no is understood by the young adolescent, and frequently, where the relationship is good enough, that urgent plea will be largely heeded.

THEIR FIRST EXPERIMENTS

Despite all your reasoned efforts, you should be prepared for some experimentation by your adolescent, even if it is quite limited. Recent studies show that virtually all adolescents have one session of heavy drinking during high school, and at least 80 percent try marijuana before they have graduated from high school. Such experimenting is not in itself too disturbing, and very often parents never know it has happened. But if you do find out, it is important for a number of reasons that you respond to it.

Indeed, if you learn about it, it is probably because your child wants you to find out. He is giving you an unconscious call for help. He himself is disturbed by what has happened and wants your guidance, though he is unable to go to you and speak directly about what he's done. He also wants your forgiveness.

This puts you in something of a sticky position, of wanting to respond to your child's need but also wanting to let him know that you consider drugs and alcohol serious issues.

I think you can manage both.

If you smell marijuana on the child's clothes or in his hair, or can see that he is wobbly and smelling of alcohol after a party, address the situation in a straightforward way, as calmly as possible. "Look, it's clear that you've been drinking and you're loaded. We've talked about this, and I want to be able to trust you."

I believe in giving a warning the first time. So you would continue: "Don't do it again. If you do"—then fill in the blank with a reasonable penalty. Something like docking your child from all activities for two weeks would probably be suitable.

Also let your adolescent know how disappointed you are in him: "I expected more from you. I thought you were a better person than this, that we could trust you. I can't tell you how disappointed I am in you." Those are strong words, and they can reach deep. The guilt they will probably induce can be extremely important in shaping your child's attitude toward drinking.

Let your child tell you as much as he wants about what happened. It is clear that you don't approve, but don't be too harsh and judgmental this first time, or he won't talk to you again about such important stuff. He will be too intimidated.

This may or may not be the best time to discuss what's happened; perhaps you'll want to wait until the next day. But by all means, let your child know that you have serious concerns. Drugs and alcohol are dangerous to the mind and body. You have tried to get him to understand that.

If you give a warning and a threat of punishment for the next time and your child breaks the rules again, you must follow through, or your credibility will be undermined.

Many parents don't respond to this first experiment or to others because, sadly, they don't want to have confrontations with their increasingly independent and potentially explosive adolescents. They deny the experiment and continue to deny the evidence. Their children may start to have difficulties at school, with a sudden drop in grades and in attendance—two of the earliest signs. Or the adolescents may exhibit a loss of appetite and weight, bloodshot eyes, stretches of lethargy and fatigue, possibly periods of hyperactivity—all signs of drug and alcohol abuse. These parents' homes may smell of marijuana smoke, a strong and unmistakable odor. But faced with all this evidence, they deny their children's drug use.

I do not believe in the laissez-faire style of parenting. When I hear a mother, for example, say something like, "I'm giving my kid her own space," I usually conclude that this is a person who is avoiding her responsibility as the parent of an adolescent. She may have complex reasons for her own behavior: perhaps, as mentioned, she fears a confrontation with her daughter; perhaps she's reacting against an overly repressive adolescence of her own; perhaps she's frustrated with her own life and projecting wishes for freedom onto her daughter. One or all of the above, it doesn't matter. The result is the same, in my view—avoidance of responsibility as the parent of an adolescent.

One father told me he did get somewhat concerned when he realized that his fifteen-year-old son was spending practically all his time at home behind the locked door of his bedroom, and that whenever the young man did come out, he seemed disconnected, high. For reasons the man could not fully explain, neither he nor his wife responded to this situation. In fact, the two of them were extremely narcissistic, extremely self-involved in their own insatiable business and social lives. Only when their son's school threatened to expel him unless he received immediate treatment for drug abuse did they finally begin to look at what they had been avoiding.

Denial is dangerous. If you don't respond to drug or alcohol use in the years from twelve to fifteen, you will allow the abusive pattern to take shape. When your child becomes sixteen, you begin to lose control, and as with sexual activities, there is much that happens of which you have no knowledge. You must have faith that the information you have provided, the model you have been, and the relationship you have built with your adolescent are sufficient to help her resist the temptations of drugs and alcohol.

COPING

There is a difference between the occasional user of drugs and/or alcohol and the chronic abuser of these substances. An occasional user smokes a joint or has a couple of drinks at weekend parties. I don't recommend that you condone such behavior, for these substances are toxic, and their use can lead to destructive behavior. If you detect even limited use, I think you have to respond—immediately and firmly—for all the reasons noted above.

Heavy usage, by which I mean daily usage, is considerably

more dangerous and most commonly derives from dysfunctional families. Unlike casual use, which can be hidden, serious abuse will usually reveal itself. A parent may well find drugs or at least evidence of them in an adolescent's room or in his pockets when picking up clothes to be cleaned. Usually, there will be a drop in school performance, as noted earlier, and it may be accompanied by a sudden change in friends and activities. Favorite sports and hobbies no longer matter. There may also be a wave of mood swings, highs and lows, and a lot of anger and irritability that seem to come from nowhere.

There are some who advocate dealing with this crisis yourself, especially if you catch the problem early. Suspending privileges—no socializing, no car—and giving only a minimal allowance are all recommended as terms of the punishment. When you see a change in behavior and are convinced that the drugs are gone, the punishment is lifted.

I'm skeptical that such an approach will be sufficient. I think most parents will need some counseling, which they can find through their family doctor or through the adolescent's school.

To begin with, heavy users are exceedingly clever at deceiving others. "It really was no big deal. I just got into it a little bit, and I promise, I'm out of it. I'll never do it again." Their reassuring patter often is what parents want to hear, giving them a way to avoid a difficult confrontation. They become what drug professionals call "enablers," unconscious colluders with their drug-abusing adolescents.

A professional experienced in drug treatment can warn parents to expect such tactics and others from their adolescent and can help them summon the emotional strength they need to deal with this terrible problem. They will learn, for example, that they must be very direct, clear, and confrontational with their adolescent. Though it will not be easy, they have to be firm and consistent, and get their young abuser into a drug prevention and detoxification program. This program might consist of daily sessions at a clinic established for adolescent drug abusers, or even residential treatment in a special drug facility for a period of weeks or months.

These treatment programs are essentially educational. Users learn about and come to accept the dangers of drugs and accept abstinence as their only option. They are strongly supported in this behavior by their peers in the program and by the attending drug professionals. At the same time, they are kept off drugs. The hope is that the combination of education, support, and detoxification will enable the adolescent to return to his daily life and to the outside world and stay clean.

Adolescent drug and alcohol abuse is a parent's most hideous nightmare, which of course is why so many parents choose to deny the problem when it first surfaces. If instead you can respond strongly to those first signs, your chances of coping and keeping the problem from growing are greatly increased.

Guiding adolescents and coping in this area is tough and very stressful for parents. Having parents as your allies can help greatly. For if you are able to talk to others who are in the same boat, you can gain strength and insight from their experiences, both good and bad.

You can also be vigilant together. If a party or dance is coming up, or your adolescent wants to join a group headed for some club on Saturday night, your job as a parent is to try to decide whether the activity is acceptable for your child. This task will be much simpler if you can compare notes with other parents you trust. Who among you has found out exactly what will be going on at this party? Will there be an adult present? If the kids want to go to a club, what sort of place is it and what kind of crowd will it attract? Will alcohol be sold to underage teens, even if IDs are required?

Once you and some other parents have agreed on a position to take toward the activity—yes or no—you can tell your adolescent that the parents of Samantha, Lauren, and Alison feel exactly the same way about this.

A network of parents might be formed informally through phone conversations, or it might be an extension of a parents association that meets periodically at one home or another. These groups can be valuable. Not only will you have a chance to see how others are coping, but you can learn about resources that might be useful: a new book on adolescents and drug problems, perhaps, or a counselor who has been especially effective with adolescents and their families.

And, of course, these groups can provide personal support. You need that. You need all you can get for this emotionally wrenching aspect of adolescence.

5

Self-Esteem: The Bedrock of Confidence and Competence

It is difficult to overemphasize the importance of feeling good about yourself when you're an adolescent. To be sure, such feelings are psychologically enhancing at any time, but for the adolescent, self-esteem can become a center of gravity. It can provide her the balance and the inner strength to withstand unhealthy peer pressures, or the need to perform in damaging ways to make herself acceptable.

Self-esteem gives adolescents the strength to act independently and take intelligent risks, to accept challenges and extend themselves in ways that allow for emotional growth, achievement, and success—developments which in turn create greater self-esteem.

Erik Erikson spoke of the latency years from around seven to ten as the age of initiative, a time when the child is exploring and experimenting, discovering himself physically, emotionally, and intellectually.

What is critical, Erikson observed, is that the child emerges from these years with enough of a sense of self to feel that in some respects he is able. Not just good, but able.

Whether this feeling of competence develops has much to do with the parents. Children, especially in latency, must feel they are appreciated. If you're going to discipline your children and criticize them, you must also find something about them to praise.

You don't have to lie. Children detect false praise quickly. And you don't have to be overly effusive. But when they do something well, encourage it even if it isn't exactly what you had in mind. You wanted her to play the piano, and she took to the flute. Nevertheless, if you like what you hear, tell her when she finishes practicing, "That was sounding good. You're really starting to get onto that piece."

In latency, children begin to develop problems of self-esteem around failing and not doing well. A six-year-old is so omnipotent and so narcissistic, so full of self in a childish way, that problems of failure don't really register. But the klutzy kid of ten who is not doing well in school can already be feeling down about himself, already thinking of himself as a failure for life. One of the reasons psychiatrists become so concerned about learning disabilities during latency has little to do with the learning disability itself. It has to do with the attendant loss of self-esteem, especially for bright children in families where doing well in school is extremely important.

SUPPORT THEIR STRENGTHS

A child's self-esteem is also affected by ambitions his parents hold for him. If he is the best basketball player in his school, but his parents have always dreamed of raising a concert violinist, he might still end up not feeling very good about himself.

By the time a child is ten or eleven years old, it's important for his parents to support those activities in which he is adept and to follow the child's lead. If his strength really lies in basketball, and he continues to struggle hopelessly and joylessly with the fiddle, perhaps it's time to drop the violin lessons. I have seen many families in which the matter of options is carried too far. Exposing children between the ages of six and eight to a variety of activities from painting classes to gymnastics can broaden them and reveal their talents and interests. But there comes a point where the child can simply be overloaded, and where the lack of talent and/or interest in an activity should be recognized and conceded by the parents.

This not to suggest that you simply ignore those areas where a child is struggling. It depends on the problem. If, for example, the child has difficulty with English, that is a problem that could plague her throughout her educational career. It could also be a perpetual source of low self-esteem. In such a case, you might well explore the difficulties with your child and her teachers, making it a problem you are trying to grapple with alongside her. Then, perhaps, a tutor and encouragement can restore self-esteem.

Improved grades in English will obviously help, for she will proudly realize that they are a result of her own extra effort. And so will the parental attitude of "do your best," a sincere expression by you that so long as she tries her best, she's doing okay. If instead you retain unrealistically high standards in English for your child, standards she is incapable of achieving, then anything less and her self-esteem will be undermined. But if she can raise her English to the level, say, of "average student" in her class, and you applaud her for it, her positive feelings about herself will increase. She will feel that she may not be the best in her class, but she is still "adequate," and that is light-years better than being at the bottom of her class.

SINKING TO THE LOWEST LEVEL

There is a special danger to be avoided here. Children know if they are good or bad at something. If your child reaches the age of thirteen or fourteen and you are still holding out academic goals for him that are well beyond his reach, not only will he feel himself to be a failure, he will seek out others who share an unconscious lack of self-esteem.

Parents often ask me about steering their children away from bad kids, but they don't usually recognize that they can quite unknowingly push their children toward bad kids by undermining their self-esteem. Once a child feels that way, he will seek the company of those he is comfortable with. They support one another, and they help one another feel better.

Unfortunately, this often takes the form of antisocial behavior. In some cases, they improve their feelings about themselves by stealing something beautiful or taking money. Much truancy behavior and a certain amount of drug behavior, especially the taking up of drugs and smoking in the first place, stem from an effort to shore up weak self-esteem.

To some degree, self-esteem is defined by the culture. If using drugs and having problems in school are valued by a culture, or a subset of that culture into which a young adolescent has dropped, his behavior will be affected accordingly. Among such peers, being the smartest student in the school brings abuse, not admiration.

It can be extremely difficult for an adolescent to resist the culture—to be the only member of her group, say, not to smoke—especially if her self-esteem is shaky and largely dependent on acceptance by the others.

But with the kind of parental awareness I described, an adolescent should be able to develop the strength to resist in such situations. Children can come out of latency with a sense of satisfaction about themselves and about their abilities. Not that they will feel transcendent, the best in everything. But they can possess a reasonable sense of their own intellect, that they are smart enough to satisfy themselves. And they can feel comfortable with their physical abilities, that there are one or two sports at which they are pretty good. And, importantly, they can feel reasonably good about their bodies.

PROBLEMS WITH BODY IMAGE

Feelings about body image profoundly affect both girls and boys. Indeed, I have found this issue to be so critical to the healthy development of adolescents that twice I stepped beyond the usual boundaries of psychiatry to recommend plastic surgery.

Both patients were young women. After treating them for some time, it was clear that each suffered psychologically because of their physical attributes. One had an extremely large nose, the other extremely large breasts. Our psychotherapy sessions were full of comments on self-loathing. "I feel so ugly. I feel as if everyone is always staring at me," said the girl with the large nose. The other said things like, "Boys are always pushing into me. One boy actually asked me, in front of everyone, 'Hey, how can you walk without falling over?' and all his friends just stood there laughing."

These were clearly severe body-image problems rooted in reality, quite different from the vision an anorexic has of herself of always being too fat, even when in fact she resembles a prisoner at Auschwitz. So, while we worked in psychotherapy on the related psychic blows and pain these adolescents were suffering, I decided to review their cases with a plastic surgeon at my hospital. His experience with such cases, he told me, was quite positive.

I then talked with the girls and their parents about the possibility of such surgery, taking great care not to give them unrealistic hopes. They would not become movie stars overnight, I cautioned them, nor would their personalities change with the operations. Each adolescent carried psychological problems she had brought into therapy. Some, but not all, were related to body image. So while the body-image issues might be ameliorated with plastic surgery, I told them, and presumably they would no longer have to suffer the daily reslashing of their wounds, which in itself should diminish their psychological problems, they would still remain the same people.

On careful balance and with reasonable perspective, then, they chose surgery. In both cases, there were dramatic, sudden changes in their self-esteem.

It was only two cases, to be sure, and I would never casually propose such an approach to therapy. But these two cases were wonderfully positive.

FINDING DESIRABLE PEERS

Children who enter adolescence with confidence and competence, with the feeling that they've got something to hold their head up for, find it easier to fit within a peer group that is suitable for them.

For example, young men with a higher sense of their intellectual abilities are drawn to peers who value this quality, and who do not find athletics, perhaps, to be very meaningful. This peer group may then join the group of likeminded individuals who put out the student literary magazine.

A kind of comfort index evolves. Often quite unconsciously, young adolescents sense and avoid those areas that might lower their self-esteem. A boy might have played a certain amount of football before high school and enjoyed it. But now he knows he is not good enough and/or big enough to make the team. So his serious football days are over. He might still play the game, but now it's a pickup game with friends, two-handed tag on a Saturday morning. Now he plays only for fun and so acquires a fuller, more realistic perspective on himself and the adjusted place of sports in his changing life.

He begins to narrow his interests to other areas of competence, begins to focus on those activities where he can perceive possibilities of success. Perhaps this is when he tries out for the school newspaper as a sportswriter. He has always been a better writer than football player anyway, he knows, so maybe he can write about the sport. On the newspaper, of course, he will find people like himself, and they will become his clique. Certainly, by the time he is fifteen or sixteen, he ought to be part of a small clique who spend a fair amount of time shoring up one another's self-esteem, one another's egos.

Cliques of this sort become his natural habitat and last through his college/late-adolescent days. By then, the lines are more clearly drawn: there are intellectual peer groups, athletic groups, fraternities, and other social groups. And though there is obviously some crossing of lines, they are largely separate worlds.

Around the time the young man decided to give up football for the newspaper, the system was beginning to make such decisions for him. It told him he simply wasn't good enough for the football team. The days of lower school and junior high when everybody got to play were over. The culture, in other words, encourages a certain amount of specialization.

Such specialization becomes more apparent by the time he's in college, when he is faced with the choice of a major, which is a way to make people focus on their strengths. By this point, the student should have completed one of the key tasks of adolescence: he should have developed an adequate sense of himself as a person who is quite acceptable to a particular peer group. And to some degree, his choice of his major is a choice of peer groups. He knows what he is best at, and by the last years of college, that knowledge should be integrated with his choice of a clique.

The peers in this clique, being segregated, reassure one another of their worthiness. The writers on a college campus, for example, may be on the margins of the larger society, but they support one another, their position, their self-esteem.

They also become important supporters in another adolescent struggle, the struggle for sexual identity. These peers can affirm for one another that they are sexually okay, that they have solidified their sexual identity as a male or a female.

WHEN PARENTS IGNORE
AND WITHHOLD

In my practice, I have seen a number of parents who were so tied up in their own narcissistic needs that they ignored the basics of parenting. These were not evil people. But they were so involved in their own careers and their own divorces, so self-involved, that their children simply were not high priorities for them. They had money and they gave their children that. But they did not give— were incapable of giving—their children much of themselves.

Parenting for me means providing adequate guidance and support where and when it is needed. That's what these people were never able to give their children, not when the children were younger, not when they were adolescents. And by not providing that, these parents virtually guaranteed low self-esteem for their children.

There are countless other ways that a child can end up with low self-esteem. For example, Heinz Kohut, who expanded upon Freud to develop self-psychology, speaks of links to infancy, and of what happens if the infant does not receive from her parents the love and attention she needs to create a basis upon which to build self-esteem. Instead of that foundation, the emotionally neglected child has a hole. It is a hole that a person can spend a lifetime trying to fill.

Or, in adolescence, a child of extremely accomplished parents may feel intellectually inferior to them. I encounter this among the children of professors. They feel they can't live up to their parents and the expectations they imagine their parents have for them. Since these expectations are often their own inner distortions, therapy is useful to these children—by revealing their distortions and allowing them to comprehend and accept that in reality less is demanded of them than they had imagined. In other words, they are themselves quite accomplished, they are themselves good kids, and they are themselves loved and appreciated by their parents.

Or a boy may be uncoordinated. He can't play basketball, baseball, any sports. He can't compete physically in society, and we live in a society that values such abilities. Quite understandably, he will not feel very good about himself. His parents and teachers can attempt to alter such a self-image by pointing out to him the other good qualities he has. And, they hope, he will go through a few experiences that confirm what they say.

The son of a friend of mine was once in just such a state. She and her husband tried to tell him that it didn't really matter that he was awkward and a bad athlete because he was terrific in many other ways, including being a very good student. Not surprisingly, they were not very effective. He did know that his parents at least loved him and did not think badly of him because he couldn't hit a baseball to save his life. But meanwhile, he was convinced that his peers thought he was a nerd.

Then one day, his whole life changed. He came home and jubilantly told his mother that his class had had its first spelling competition. "Mom," he said, beaming, "everybody wanted me on their team." That was only the beginning. Subsequently, whenever there were spelling bees and other intellectual competitions, his classmates fought over who could get him on their side. And as academic accomplishment in general became more important to him and his peers, he became an increasingly respected member of his class.

I should mention one special pitfall for parents in this particular struggle. From around the age of seven, children begin to compare themselves to their peers, and by the time they are twelve, how they feel they match up against their peers, how they feel their peers think of them are more important to them than what their parents seem to think of them.

That's why a parent with the most loving intentions and a full share of honesty may very well not be believed by an adolescent when the parent earnestly insists, "But you're not stupid. Okay, so you didn't get an A in math. You got a C. But math is very tough for you. There's no disgrace in that. What matters is that you gave it your best shot. Keep working hard, and you'll do better. Don't worry about it. You got an A in English, and that's fabulous—okay, so an A-minus. And a B in French—right, a B-plus—which is also fabulous. So don't put yourself down for math. Keep doing your best, that's all I ask. Who cares if you don't go to MIT? Who cares if you're not going to win a Nobel Prize in physics? Just do your best, and you will do fine."

These remarks are absolutely true, splendidly supportive, and include very good advice. And the fretting adolescent hears them. But what he also hears is his own inner voice, which is saying something like: "Yeah, yeah, yeah. Meanwhile, I got a C, and Ben got a B, and Christian got an A. Let's face it, my mother says all that because that's her job. Like, she's my *mother,* dude."

We live in a competitive society, and he feels he is losing the competition. But all is not lost. The unconscious hears. Even if consciously he wrestles with his mother's complimentary view of him, unconsciously he does feel her support and love. That will give him strength; that will bolster his self-esteem. Imagine what he might feel and think about himself if he got a C in math and received no balancing support from his mother. Or worse, got put down by her. What if she said instead: "How do you expect to get into *any* decent college with a C in math?"

THE PRICE OF PARENTAL DENIAL

I told you earlier about the parents who were astonished to discover, or rather to be informed by their son's school, that he was a drug addict at age fifteen. They knew the boy was spending a lot of time alone in his room, seemed listless and mildly depressed much of the time. But drugs!

These parents never talked with their son about such matters as drugs at school or his own unsteady behavior. They never even acknowledged that the smell emanating from his room was the strong, acrid scent of marijuana smoke. They never thought about it. They were that disconnected from him.

For another family, the problem was not drugs but the boy's behavior in school. He was so disruptive that the school threatened to throw him out—even though his father was a substantial contributor to the school's fund drives—if the family didn't get help for the boy.

The father's attitude was largely one of denial. "There's nothing much wrong with my son," he told me. "He's just a chip off the old block. When I was that age, I was in trouble all the time at school. But since the school insists, well, fix him up, Doc. Tone him down a little." Basically, he told me, give him an oil job and a little wax, and send him on his way.

The man and his wife were divorcing, with a vengeance, and I told them both that I needed to work with them and the boy in order to accomplish anything. And that's true. Unless I can get the parents involved in cases like this, there isn't much I can do. They both said, "Of course."

But every time I tried to get them into my office, they made excuses. The father would say he was flying off to Berlin, and the mother would give her own explanations. "My grandmother has TB and is about to die in South Dakota," she once actually told me, explaining why she couldn't come to my office that day. But when the boy arrived, he told me that she had an appointment at Elizabeth Arden. Their basic attitude was that if there was a problem with their son, I should fix it and give them a call when everything was better. Meanwhile, they certainly would be glad to pay for whatever was needed.

I had the boy tested and learned that he was dyslexic, that he reversed letters and numbers when he read. The school had been unsuccessfully trying to help the boy by getting the parents sufficiently concerned to at least have him tested. When we finally ran the tests, we discovered that at the age of fourteen, he could barely read or write.

When I informed his mother that he would need special tutoring, she said, "Goodness, Doctor, I had no idea." When she went on to tell me, "Okay, just get a tutor," I felt the same way their cook must feel when she reports a broken stove.

I witnessed another case of neglect in which the parents gave their son money but nothing of themselves. So he found his own way to develop the self-esteem they had deprived him of. He became a drug dealer at his private school.

The role brought him a tremendous amount of prestige. In a sense, he was showing his friends that he was the best at defying the authorities of the school. At last, there was something at which he could excel, and for which many of his peers gave him credit. Before that, no one had ever helped that boy feel there was anything of value about himself, that he could do much of anything well.

These cases all involved wealthy families. Giving the children money made it easier for the parents to rationalize their own neglectful behavior.

But the same behavior and results can be found in families who are not wealthy. Parents don't have to be rich to ridicule their children or not take the children and their ambitions seriously. They don't have to be rich to convey to their children that they really don't have much time for them or much interest in their problems and their lives. They don't have to be rich to be always finding fault with their children.

By not parenting, by not emotionally supporting their children or applauding them, by not reassuring them that they are competent and achievers, any parents, rich or poor, can contribute to the development of children with holes in them where their self-esteem should be.

The results are tragic.

6

Identity and Separation: Disruptions and Opportunities

One of the great quests of the adolescent is the search for self-identity, the unconscious pursuit of a character, personality, and being that the adolescent feels are his own, rather than merely reflections of his parents.

Implicit in this search is a separation from parents. This almost inevitable process is normally rocky for parents, but with awareness, they can avoid turning their relationship with their restless adolescent into a fierce tug-of-war.

As a matter of fact, there are great opportunities for parents during this time. It is a period of both emotional and intellectual growth, when the child for the first time becomes capable of abstract thinking. The blending of these elements—his quest for self-identity and his intellectual development—allows him to reevaluate any number of ideas, beliefs that he had simply accepted before, that he had indeed been incapable of examining before. Moral, political, and religious positions are frequently among them. If the child takes a new stand, it can become a point of contention between him and his parents, especially when the parents feel a new argumentativeness and are unaware of its roots. As we'll see, this same growth and searching offer a special chance for parents to stimulate and guide their adolescent in very significant new ways.

A TENTATIVE BEGINNING

The process starts in the latency years, when the child begins in a most tentative way to establish differences between himself and his parents. As noted, we frequently see such differences in the child's choice of cultural heroes, film and television favorites, and especially in the choice of music. At the same time, he is reaching out, testing himself and life to find those areas where he can do well. It might be as a baseball player, a writer, an actor, or a guitar player; whatever allows him to start feeling good about himself.

As that achievement is verified by his parents, his sense of self-competence grows, and in general his self-confidence blossoms. He carries this feeling with him into adolescence, and there it provides a foundation from which he can reach out and further test his abilities.

As these feelings of competence and confidence continue to build, the young adolescent begins to say to himself, "I'm okay. I'm pretty good at sports, at English, at art. People like me. I'm a pretty good person." And unconsciously these feelings fuel the idea that "I can be a good person with interests of my own, a person who's different from other people, certainly different from my parents."

The need for appreciation and approval from parents diminishes. Meaningful approval increasingly comes from peers. In addition, the unconscious drive toward maturation found in the playing out of the Oedipal issue leads to separation: the incest barrier increases the adolescent's need to distance himself from his parents. There is almost a biological mandate to be different.

Indeed, the hallmark of the psychological adolescent is when he becomes different from his parents, when he begins to develop significant and serious interests that are not those of his parents.

This development, around the ages of fourteen to sixteen, is the beginning of the divorce of the adolescent from the adult. It's not necessarily a divorce from the values of the parents; in a strong family, those values will be retained. But his perspective becomes increasingly his own. With different interests, different opinions, a different view of the world, he begins to solidify his sense that he is an individual, truly separate from his parents.

A LEAP TO ABSTRACTIONS

Until now, the child's mental abilities were largely limited to concrete operations. She absorbed facts and reasoned on the basis of facts. Adding, subtracting, doing word problems. Most issues in life were either black or white, good or bad, right or wrong. (Organized religions are effective with children in part because they teach precepts that are clear and unequivocal.) Quite consistently, she perceived her parents as all-powerful and all-knowing. If they were Republicans, then the Republicans were the good guys.

With the ability to think abstractly, which develops around the ages of thirteen to fifteen, the young adolescent begins to discern grays, and for the first time she thinks about subjects for herself. Accepted certainties are reexamined.

She reexamines her own values, for example, and compares them with those of her parents. This usually leads to her questioning her parents in a new way. Up to now, her parents could do no wrong. But now, the adolescent can begin to see that her parents are not perfect and omniscient after all. They may not even be able to answer questions in her math homework. She begins to recognize her parents' failings, as well as their successes. She realizes that they can be mistaken. She begins to establish her own positions: "Just because they are Republicans doesn't mean I have to be one."

In all likelihood, she won't come to that conclusion quietly. Most likely, she will test out her theory, her discovery, in a challenging discussion. Most likely, it will be a discussion to which she will bring a certain amount of heat. This is the process of adolescence.

Of course, this passion is not connected to the issues or principles or candidates of one political party as compared with another. Rather it may well flow from her recognition that her parents are not perfect. That realization can be upsetting for two reasons. It means her parents are not the omnipotent protectors and providers she—and all children—fantasize them to be, want them to be. It also means that if she is going to act upon her disagreement with her parents, if she is going to be a liberal to oppose their conservatism, she must act on her own. While this is clearly a chance to assert herself, to establish her own identity, it is also a moment of opposing her parents, of standing on her own, and that can be unnerving.

What a parent experiences, then, is a discussion that starts with some welcome questions about politics and soon escalates to a passionate attack. Rational? No. Adolescence? Yes.

This "growth of abstraction," as the psychologist Jean Piaget called it, opens up the possibility of significant reevaluations in a number of areas besides politics.

Religion, for example. When the child was ten, she accepted whatever her parents told her, and her vision of God was a man with a big white beard sitting up on a cloud. By the time she is fifteen, she might have a much more diffused naturalistic view: God is an essence of the spirit of oneness with the world and is not some superperson sitting up there on a cloud passing judgments.

Perhaps her parents are believing Catholics. Now she becomes quite aware that not everyone in her class is Catholic; many are, say, Jewish. And she begins to wonder and talk with them about Judaism. Maybe, she thinks, there is another religion that makes more sense to me than what I grew up with.

This is obviously another potential hot spot. Religiously mixed marriages are glowing targets for this kind of questioning. However, with some awareness of what their adolescent is going through, parents can use this sort of discussion to foster an important principle of adolescence: we can disagree, hold quite different views, yet still love one another.

Respect and honesty matter here. In a discussion of religion, parents may uphold their own views and their desires to see their adolescent continue in the religion she was raised, while allowing that as she gets older, she might find herself making a different choice. Mixed marriages symbolically represent the acceptance of different views, the transcendence of love, all of which can be pointed out in the discussion.

This great awakening of the adolescent can be trying for parents. Not only are many of their long-held views suddenly being questioned and devalued by their child, and done so rather passionately, but their authority is being questioned as well. Whereas a parent of a ten-year old was a hero, the parent of a fifteen-year-old has clay feet.

A NEW ROLE IN THE FAMILY

The search for self-identity also gets played out in the adolescent's position in the family. In countless everyday ways, this position will shift from that of subservient child to equal or near-equal adult.

The child of nine or ten bends entirely to the authority and orders of his parents. These are often connected to family rituals: what time the family sits down for dinner, what time the child is expected to go to bed. But the searching adolescent begins to define the degree to which he will collaborate in the family position that has been silently assigned to him.

I spoke earlier of the importance of limits and structure in the family and noted that both could be elements of negotiation as adolescence evolves. This reaching for a new position in the family is a good example of what I meant.

Perhaps the first of these rituals to go, to be claimed in the search, is the nightly bath. The bath is overthrown for the shower. Furthermore, no one is allowed to check out the results. And maybe the time shifts to the morning. These are mild enough assertions, but they matter to the child.

The child also wants to set his own bedtime. At first, this is a request, and he bases his argument on how much later his friends are permitted to stay up. Then, around ages fourteen to fifteen, bedtime becomes a function of what must be done at night. Homework must be done. A certain amount of talking on the phone—perhaps agreed upon—must be done. On some nights, certain agreed-upon programs must be watched on TV. On weekends, many parents deliberately keep bedtime flexible. Go to bed when you feel like going to bed, they tell them, watch *Saturday Night Live* until one in the morning if you want. So a degree of independence is acknowledged.

Sitting down for family dinner at seven might still be expected. This special time when the whole family is together can become ever more important, a time when adolescent issues can be discussed and negotiated. Increasingly, however, the teenager will impose his autonomy here as well. Halfway through the meal he announces that he has too much homework tonight, may he be excused? Or she has a huge exam the next day and doesn't feel like eating at all. On weekends, dates and parties will change everything, often taking precedence over family dinner and other family plans. A big party has to be factored into the whole family's calendar. Maybe that weekend, the family cannot plan to visit friends in the country.

What is unfolding through this series of shifts, through this growing autonomy, is his changing role in the family—from subservient child to near-equal adult. (I qualify the term because I don't think a daughter or son ever becomes a true equal in the eyes of the parents, even when the child is fifty years old.)

The change over these years is meaningful. And even though, as I suggested, much of it is played out subtly with a kind of natural rhythm to it, there are obviously many opportunities for confrontation over authority.

To me, this is yet another opportunity or series of opportunities to increase your parental fund of psychological credit. There can be years of skirmishes over relatively minor issues. Or you can deliberately concede the little skirmishes to better win the big ones. If you are, in other words, responsive to your child's search for autonomy, and let him know that you are—"Okay, you're old enough to decide for yourself how late you have to stay up to get everything done"—that will register with him.

A parent who understands her child will earn his trust, and he will respond to the parent's needs on other issues in return.

AN EDUCATIONAL
OPPORTUNITY

Your child's new capacity for abstract thinking allows him to think in more complex terms and to absorb a whole new world of data. This development can present a great opportunity for you as an educator. You can encourage questioning, stimulate interests, explore issues where there are subtleties.

For the first time, you may be able to discuss human relationships as complex involvements in which people who love each other can also hurt each other. You may begin to have a context for talk about sex in a relationship, how one hopes it's more than a brief physical satisfaction, a sensual fling. That's an important idea for an adolescent to understand, one that might affect the teenager's own attitude toward sex. But until now, it was beyond him.

Why were we in Vietnam? The abstractions of such a complicated war can now be approached. Were we right in our actions? Does that mean the United States is not always automatically right?

Television serves a new purpose, and its usual simplistic one-dimensional offerings can provide a daily agenda: Another bomb from the IRA? What are they fighting about all this time in Ireland? Why do the Serbs hate the Bosnians so, and what does "ethnic cleansing" mean?

In general, there is a passion at this age for learning of all kinds. It is as if the young adolescent discovers a wonderful new tool and can't get enough use out of it.

Timing matters. Parents who can connect with this passion and feed it, exposing their child to stimulating and enriching experiences, can meaningfully affect their child's intellectual development.

A KEY TO REAL LEARNING

This period of intellectual awakening among children is especially significant to parents who have above-average ambitions for their children.

By and large, the educational system in our society is designed to meet society's goals, and they may not be the ones you hold for your child. Our educational system is geared toward educating blue-collar or white-collar workers, not writers and artists and doctors and lawyers and architects. So if a realistic assessment of your child's abilities and talents leads you to have more ambitious goals for her, the burden is on you to help her realize her potential. There are two important steps you can take.

The first is to provide the child with a highly stimulating home environment, and this begins long before adolescence or even latency. It starts with reading to your child when she is two, conveying to her your own pleasure with books. Reading regularly to your child allows her to develop her own interest in books and to associate reading with a special benefit—time alone with Mommy or Daddy.

As she grows up, she will receive subtle supportive messages if yours is a home where books and good music are valued, where trips to art, historical, and other museums are enjoyed, where good theatrical shows are special treats.

This stimulating environment should also communicate a sense of human possibility—evidenced by the artistic and intellectual accomplishments she is exposed to—one that silently suggests to her the idea that she can become anything she wants.

The second step is to search out the special school that will complement your home environment and nurture your goals. This might be a particular school within the public system or a private school, perhaps one that offers financial aid to make the move possible.

If you can take these two steps, which may indeed require extra work and ingenuity on your part, you will greatly increase your chances of reaching your special goals for your child. You will also increase the chances for your child to acquire "inner-directed" qualities, which I think are keys to learning and true success in school.

"Inner-directed" is a concept from sociologist David Riesman. Most people in our culture, he observed, are other-directed. They depend on the approval of others. The work they choose, the kinds of lives they lead are largely shaped by this need and the generally materialistic goals of our culture.

But others are able to respond to their own inner goals and satisfactions. They might work and live in ways that are very different from those of the great majority, yet they are unconcerned by that. They are not, for example, pursuing careers in which a great part of their motivation is to receive approval of others and large financial rewards. They are painting or writing, perhaps, or pursuing lonely scientific quests principally to satisfy themselves.

A key to real learning lies in developing the inner-directed quality of love of learning.

Back in latency, a period of great curiosity, children explore and learn if they're encouraged, and that satisfies their natural curiosity. But they are also driven by a strong desire to please their parents with good grades.

Hopefully, as they go through the school system, their gratification in learning will shift from external to internal gratification. In other words, by the time they leave high school, their drive will be to please themselves, not their parents or their peers, by learning and doing well in school.

The majority of people never actually reach this point. They go right through college with a strong component of their psychology linked to pleasing their parents, and with their own personal goals largely defined in fairly limited other-directed, materialistic ways: what has their local culture established as worthwhile?

Others are self-driven, with a great inner love for learning, with an ambition to pursue work that extends and gratifies themselves. This very special quality grows out of a family and a home environment where learning is highly valued and inner-directed ambitions are nurtured.

7

The Limits of Parental Power

This new development can be difficult and frightening for parents. Some parents simply have a hard time releasing control, giving up power. For others, just when it would seem their child needs their guidance more than ever, their control appears to be eroding.

I think it's worth looking at this shift of power, at what parental options remain, at what natural, unexpected limits evolve, at what become power struggles, and at the price of certain kinds of "victories."

Parents who understand this process stand a good chance of avoiding a number of damaging and unnecessary battles and instead can seize the opportunity to raise their relationship with their adolescent to a more adult level, which, like it or not, is the direction in which it is headed.

The older your adolescent becomes, the more you must appeal to his or her rational mind.

THREE MEANINGFUL CONTROLS

There are three levers of control that parents retain over their adolescent child. They are powerful levers, and they are easily abused.

The first is docking, the limiting of privileges. This is the least severe form of discipline, suitable for minor problems. For example, when there is continued rudeness by a brother to a sister, or when foul language is used repeatedly despite warnings, you might limit the use of the telephone or the time spent watching TV. With adolescents who have their driver's license, you can restrict the use of the family car.

More extreme is grounding, cutting off your child from his peers, shutting down his social life altogether for a period of time. To adolescents, grounding is a kind of house arrest, and it can be extremely painful. They cannot see their friends. Their own private, bubbling social existence is taken away. Perhaps the grounding was for a violation of the agreed-upon social rules, coming home from a party after midnight. Perhaps it stems from an upsetting report from school, repeated acting up with a few friends in music class. Whatever the cause, it is wise to be realistic when applying this punishment. If the grounding sentence is too long—probably more than a week or two—you will be nurturing a deep sense of injustice and resentment that will likely fester and grow and ultimately erupt into fights.

The third and potentially most damaging lever is economic discipline. If you cut your adolescent's allowance, you not only limit her activities but you remind her of just how dependent she still remains on your largesse, no matter what she imagines to the contrary, no matter how much she is struggling to create an independent self. When applied sensibly, economic discipline can be useful and teach something of a larger lesson: if you don't obey the law, life will punish you—you will be fined.

It is also a control that lends itself to abuse, to crushing a child's spirit. I have seen a terrible range of abuse, from throwing young adolescents out of the house to denying children any financial support for college unless they went to the school of their parent's choice. Such abuse inevitably leads to fierce power struggles and the potential shredding of the family.

Although these three means of control can be effective when applied intelligently, they are all essentially reactive. You are taking something away to teach a lesson. Psychologists agree that a reactive response is never as effective as giving rewards for doing well, which can be as simple and meaningful as a kiss, a hug, a compliment.

It is also helpful to remember that the controls in themselves will not provide the balance you are seeking in your relationship with your adolescent. If your daughter is an hour late returning from a party without calling you for permission to stay longer and you ground her for the next weekend, maybe even for a whole week, she will get your message. But ultimately how she behaves socially, where she goes, who she goes with, and how long she stays will rest on her relationship with you.

She draws on discussions you've had with her about social behavior, about what you expect, about what you admit has changed since your teenage years, about intelligent limits, about the social model you present to her, about common sense. And all of that leads you to feel you can trust her.

THE SEXUALLY IMPOSING ENVIRONMENT

The widespread availability of products and messages relating to sex tends to limit a parent's power.

Is it really possible for you to censor a child who is over, say, fourteen? You can refuse to subscribe to cable TV channels that carry sleaze and soft porn. You can tell your child that you won't have that garbage in the house, and you can try to make the case that it really dehumanizes and cheapens sex.

Certainly, you can be a good model. As parents, you don't watch that stuff or rent X-rated movies. (If you do, don't let your son or daughter find out, or that will be the end of any leverage you had in this area.)

But despite the precautions you take, you know that this stuff is so pervasive in our society that somewhere, somehow—perhaps at somebody else's house when those parents are out—they will see it. Or, at the corner newsstand or the local variety and magazine store, they'll buy their own copies of *Playboy* or *Penthouse* or whatever.

In fact, a least once during adolescence, you can expect to discover his copy of *Penthouse* and/or a packet of condoms and her copy of a pornographic novel. Actually, you will discover them because unconsciously they want you to discover them. They have forgotten to hide this away in order to send you a message, one they cannot quite bring themselves to tell you directly. They want you to know where they are sexually, how they have grown, in the hope that you will be understanding and forgiving.

Certainly, by the time they are sixteen or seventeen, by which time the law admits them to almost any movie, and by which time such matters as NC-17 films and sex magazines will be fairly commonplace among their peers, censorship becomes rather nonsensical. Nevertheless, you can still determine what you will allow in your own home. You don't like the stuff, and don't want it, just as you may tell your older adolescents to watch their language, at least around you. If their adolescent friends find relentless cursing attractive, so be it; we do live in a relatively free country. But not around you, thank you.

The challenge for parents is to make their views known without seriously distancing their child and losing a sense of trust in one another. Facing reality helps here.

Some years ago, a patient told me of his experience when he was nineteen, trying to go to Europe for the summer between his sophomore and junior years in college. He had worked and saved for the trip but needed another $300, so he turned to his parents for a loan. They had given him permission for the trip, though they were not especially enthusiastic. Now they revealed why. They were concerned that he would have sex in the big, bad world of Europe, this being some time before sex among adolescents was as widespread as it is today.

The parents had never been able to talk with their son about sex, so in a sense their worry was not surprising. Yet in fact, their son was halfway through college, living away from home, and no longer a virgin. They might have faced the fact that he was on his way to adulthood and conceded that they could no longer control his sexual activities.

Instead, they tried to bribe him. Rather than lend him the $300 he needed, his father told him they would give it to him— provided he promise *not* to have sex while in Europe. The proposal was so preposterous, my patient recalled, that he had no trouble with it. He agreed and then proceeded to have the most sexually satisfying summer of his life all over the continent.

But the incident was quite damaging to the relationship between the young man and his parents. Not surprisingly, it was hardly the first time the parents had tried to control their son in an unrealistic and unreasonable manner. All through his adolescence, he had come up against their efforts, and increasingly his parents seemed to him out of touch, unfair. Increasingly, he resorted to the defense of silence. Rather than be unreasonably controlled, he stopped talking to them about nearly everything that mattered to him. He went about his life, remaining for the most part determinedly civil, but growing farther and farther apart from them. So, in a way, he was prepared for their Europe offer and dealt with it in the same way he had been dealing with them for years.

treated like a child. But there is that other, new, assertive part that says he should be entitled to the privileges of adults. As a result, you find yourself having to make new evaluations. If you ban a particular movie, are you creating the temptation for him to act out against this prohibition and go and secretly see it?

Compromise will become increasingly important. A colleague recently turned down his son's request for permission and money to go to the heavy metal concert of a group that was famous for the riots at its performances. He told his son, "No, not this time. I think at fourteen you're still a little young for that, and I don't like their reputation for riots anyway. But, maybe in a year or so, we can talk about this again."

There was an element of danger involved in attending the concert that my friend was not about to overlook. At the same time, he showed that he was willing to compromise, to remain open to the possibility that this activity would be allowed in the future. "We can talk about it next year" can become a meaningful phrase in your new dialogue with your child.

In fact your new evaluations might not be limited to a concert or an individual movie. More and more you will begin to think about what kinds of activities concern you the most, so you can use your influence and remaining power on them. More and more you will think in terms of big priorities and little priorities.

This is not a matter of drawing up a list of ten major issues and ten minor ones. Rather, it will be a reflection of a broad perspective. So, for example, issues that touch the health and safety of your child can all be considered big priorities. The rest are consigned to lesser importance.

This prioritizing elevates drug behavior, smoking, drinking, sexual behavior—and perhaps the use of a car. It can affect a decision on a heavy metal concert. It would deemphasize the controls connected with the content of movies, TV shows, the media in general. You may want to separate this control from the amount of time spent, say, watching TV. The old rule of no TV until all homework is finished need not be affected.

In some cases, as with drugs, for example, your position may be absolute: they are banned. At the same time, recognizing the realities I mentioned above, you are also educating, spreading, insofar as you can, information about the health dangers of drugs. And as for sex, total abstinence before marriage is no longer viable in our culture, but the related health issues are relevant.

In other words, even with the separation of big and little priorities, you as a parent will have decisions to make, balancing sensible use with banning, case by case.

WHEN PARENTS AND CHILD
ARE BLINDED

One of the additional effects of this major-minor approach is that it can cut down on the damaging power struggles that occur when parents are blind to the changes in their child's life and are wrestling with a naturally separating child.

These struggles can often develop over small matters, but they create tremendous friction, and they have a way of escalating. I think of the cases I've treated where this has occurred, where, for example, a seventeen-year-old finally told his parents that he has resented the way they've treated him and his TV privileges ever since he was thirteen. For four terrible years, he has suffered their insistence that he watch only on weekends, even when he had finished his homework and they were sitting in the next room audibly enjoying a TV show. Now they were all finally in my office, and I was hearing his litany of this long power struggle of which the TV limitations were part. His resentment had finally built up to an explosion and he was threatening to drop out of school. "I've had it. I'm dropping out. I'm going to get a job. Don't bother me."

I had one case recently in which the young man had announced that he was quitting high school to take the Fire Academy exam. It was his irrational declaration of independence from his very controlling parents, who had their hearts set on a good college for their only child. "I don't know what all the trouble's about," the young man said. "All I want to do is be a fireman."

The parents were so disturbed and confused, and the young man was so angry, no one could think clearly.

I pointed out to the fellow that if he were serious, he would have to complete high school. The Fire Academy, I happened to know, did not accept anyone who had not graduated from high school. It was the sort of simple fact that he would have known, too, if he had been acting in a somewhat more rational way and done the simplest research.

Separately I pointed out to his parents another simple fact known to any reader of the newspaper: at that time in New York City, because of budget limitations, students were being graduated from the Fire Academy, but they could not become active firefighters. There was a waiting list of years.

In other words, the odds were good that he would complete high school and bad that he would ever become a fireman. All of this delighted the parents. But I tried to make them understand that their son was really seventeen years old and they could no longer impose their will on him as they had been doing. He wouldn't accept it. I advised them to let him finish high school and then decide for himself what he wanted to do. He might very well want to take a year or two and work. He might then very well decide to go on to college, but the college of his choice, not theirs.

I tried to get them to understand that the alternative to their accepting this scenario was his angry behavior. His declaration about the Fire Academy was unconsciously calculated by him to punish his parents. It was an assertive, masculine declaration of independence. He was saying to them, "See what I can do, just because you want me to go and do something else."

This was a pure control struggle. In these struggles, as I have seen countless times, adolescents have an uncanny, unconscious ability to profoundly upset their parents. They come up with ideas and plans that, like large knives, pierce the hearts of their parents. Over the years, the children have absorbed the subtle dreams and hopes and plans their parents sustain for them, and those are what, in their desperation to separate, they unconsciously try to slash.

This poor seventeen-year-old was in the midst of a real struggle. The way it was headed, there would be no winners. I was able to get him and his parents refocused so they could try to work out their lives on more realistic and healthy terms, rather than the destructive struggle of who controls whom.

In other words, I was able to get them, perhaps for the first time, to negotiate and compromise.

I've had other cases where similarly struggling adolescents suddenly announced to their parents that they were dropping out of high school, typically in their last year, without even the imaginary alternative of a Fire Academy. That, of course, was tremendously disturbing to the parents, which again was very much part of the adolescent's unconscious plans.

What I've found most effective in these difficult cases is for the parents to express their concern and say something along these lines: "If you're going to do this, you've got to get a productive job, and you probably won't find one if you haven't graduated from high school. Since you're so close to that, why not finish and spend the summer trying to find a job? Then, fine, join the workforce, but we'll expect you to pay room and board here. If you earn enough to find your own place, you're free to do that if you want. . . . We still love you. We still care about you. But we still need some rules around here."

In my experience, these cases will be resolved in the natural course of events. The adolescent wins a meaningful inner battle. Then he searches for the job, and when he sees that basically what is available to him is a minimum-wage job at McDonald's, he makes the decision himself to do what society, not his parents, is now asking of him: to go to college.

There are exceptions, of course. There are countless adolescents who are not suited for college, emotionally and/or intellectually. Obviously, with such children, a parent tries to be supportive in a different way, in a way that will help the adolescent to find the job, perhaps the special training, the course in life that will be fullest and most satisfying.

I have known children of professional parents who were, for one reason or another, not meant for college. This realization came as something of a blow for them and their parents, but once they got over that, these adolescents found their own special places in life and did very well for themselves.

8

Conflicts and Negotiations

Throughout this book, I have touched on conflicts over issues of independence. These can start early over matters like bedtime and how much TV is allowed, and continue throughout adolescence, covering such issues as how late to stay out on Friday and Saturday nights, what friends are acceptable, and when the family car is available.

As I suggested in the previous chapter, these can become life-and-death struggles of control, or they can be acknowledged as matters open to discussion, compromise, and negotiation. "I disagree with you. I really think eleven o'clock is late enough for you to be out, but I must admit there are some exceptions, and this party sounds like one of them."

As a general rule, so far as these issues are concerned, I think the only occasions for significant friction are when there is danger to the adolescent or others. Then there isn't much to compromise, though even then the ruling parent can be less than brutal. The denial might be coupled with hope, for example. "You're still a little young for that. Maybe next year."

In addition to the conflicts over independence, there are wide-ranging conflicts over role identity, which encompasses all of an adolescent's personal goals: the schools she aims for, her professional ambitions, her personal future, her place in society. Conflicts around role identity can be severe, and if mishandled by parents, they can result in fierce and complete ruptures between child and family.

LEARNING TO COMMUNICATE

One of the common early role-identity conflicts surfaces over the choice of college. Typically, a parent with strong ideas and not a little of his own identity tied up in the decision attempts to bludgeon a child into a particular choice. Such an effort can easily backfire.

Quickly, the issue shifts from the advantages and suitability of one school as opposed to another. The adolescent feels challenged to assert himself, to determine his own future, and that, rather than which is the best school, becomes the issue.

When the parent in such a battle resorts to his atom bomb, the refusal to pay for any school other than his choice, he blows up the adolescent's ties to the family. The adolescent may or may not go to the imposed school. If he does, it will be in a crushed, depressed state. And the chances are good that before long he will remove himself from the continuing influence of such a dictatorial parent.

In my experience, such a disaster spills from a family in which there is generally not much communication. Throughout the application process, views on both sides should be aired. Parents should have plenty of opportunities to argue for their favorites, while their children should be able to express their own strong feelings.

But not all families can talk. I have seen families that don't talk because unconsciously the parents don't like or don't want to be close to their child. I have also seen families that don't talk because one or both of the parents are intimidated by their volatile child. Rather than facing and dealing with this problem, they unconsciously defend themselves from uncomfortable encounters by simply avoiding meaningful issues that might trigger some unpredictable, perhaps abusive response from their child.

I have seen other families in which the parents' difficulties with communication reflect other problems, such as being too busy with their own lives to give much time to their child. I call these "fix it parents" because they end up coming to me and saying, "There seems to be this problem with our child. Please fix it. Just tell us how much money you need, and fix it." They have the idea that the way to raise a child is to give it a certain amount of attention as a baby, and after that buy it what it requires, and it sort of grows up by itself. Like growing a vegetable that will thrive if they simply water it enough.

Talk does not mean manipulation, and I have seen any number of families where one is substituted for the other. One patient told me of being offered a car if he would live at home and go to a particular college nearby. It was a fine school that he had been weighing against another in a different part of the country, and part of his evaluation process was measuring the experience of living away from home. He had been undecided, but as soon as his parents offered the bribe, he knew it was time for him to get out of that house.

When the time came for me to choose a college, I had been accepted at Harvard and others, including the University of Rochester. I had never expected to be accepted by Harvard, but I had decided it was too tough for me anyway. So I rushed home and announced to my father that I was going to Rochester. My father, who I knew had considerable expectations for me, simply said, "Okay." I nearly fainted, having expected a severe lecture from him about all the sacrifices he and my mother had made in order for me to go to Harvard, et cetera, et cetera. But not a word. If we had had that pitched battle, I would surely have gone to Rochester. As it was, I could consider the matter for myself, talk with friends and faculty unburdened by the necessity to assert myself against my father. I could listen and think with a clear head, which I did, and I went to Harvard for four of the best years of my life.

Contrast that with the experience of a classmate of mine at NYU Medical School. She was a very bright student, but at the time there were still only a limited number of women going to medical school. After a year, her parents, who were wealthy and rigidly conservative, decided they didn't think she should become a doctor. Stereotypically, they told her to quit and get married and raise a family. She argued, but they refused to pay her tuition or any of her bills, so she had to leave.

Some years later, I ran into her at a medical conference. She had separated from her family, gotten a job, and earned enough in a few years to return to and complete medical school. She had also married the fellow she met during our first year in medical school. She was an M.D. with a family of her own, though still separated from her parents.

PARENTS' UNCONSCIOUS MOTIVES

What I often find at the heart of these devastating confrontations is an unconscious motive on the part of a parent. Without realizing it, the father or mother—usually the father—has strongly invested his own identity and ambitions in the child. Then the destructive pattern Anna Freud warned of, and which I mentioned earlier, begins to unfold. The child must perform according to the parent's needs and fantasies. We see this most vividly and chillingly with certain child Olympic athletes and their totally obsessed parents. But the same kind of phenomenon occurs over role-identity conflicts. So far as the parent is concerned, the child *must* attend a particular college, or in many cases, the child *must* prepare for and take over the family business.

The parent, being unaware of his own motivations, is quite blind to what is happening, unable to perceive his own intransigence and its effect on his child. The same kind of intransigence can be seen in extremely religious families when the adolescent struggling for independence shows the first signs of wavering in his faith. The parents' erupting anger and rigidity force the child to dig in his heels and take a stronger antireligious position. When I have been able to advise parents in these confrontations, I have urged them to coolly negotiate a compromise that will respect the child's need but keep him within the family and defuse the bomb. This approach allows the adolescent to work through the problem without the pressure of a confrontation, and in many cases he will find his own way back to the fold.

At New York University, I counsel medical students. I have lost track of the number of students who have come to me and said, "I'm going to quit medical school. I never wanted to be a doctor anyway. My father wanted me to be a doctor. My family made me be a doctor. I don't know what I'm doing here. I don't like it. I've finally realized this is not for me."

In some cases, the student is having a delayed identity crisis. Many adolescents go through high school rather tranquilly, and it is only in college or later that they test out how independent they are.

For others, the boredom of the first year of medical school—learning 8,424 names for parts of the anatomy and wrestling with the dreariness of biochemistry—has caused them to question their supposed desire to make sick people well.

Over and over, I have seen these students go home and announce, "I'm going to drop out of medical school. I'm going to be a . . ."

The whole issue rests very often on the parents' response. If they are able to say, "Well, you're an adult. You have to make up your own mind," the issue cools down, and the possibility of rational reexamination and discussion presents itself. Many students still take a year off from medical school to rethink their intentions, to reaffirm that this choice of profession is in fact their own, that they are really their own person. And then they return to their studies with much clearer heads.

ELEMENTS OF NEGOTIATION: DISAGREEMENT IS OKAY

I've been referring to the need for negotiation throughout this book, especially in familial conflicts over independence and role identity. In my experience, negotiation is the key to coexistence and a fairly rational adolescence.

In this section we'll review the first of three important elements of negotiation between parents and adolescents: agreeing to disagree. The other two elements—listening with respect, and graded negotiation with graded responsibility—will be covered in subsequent sections.

Learning that you can agree to disagree means that you and your child can have different tastes, can hold different opinions, different views on people and the world, and it is okay. You can still respect and love each other.

At first, such a statement might seem terribly obvious. But remember, there was a time, not so long ago, when your adolescent was really a child, barely walking, when no disagreement was allowed. You decided what she ate and when, what she wore, what she watched on TV, the music she listened to, the children she played with, the kindergarten and school she went to—everything.

Those days are gone, and with them your absolute power. Not only will your child—who is now an adolescent—increasingly differ from you and your desires, but she will increasingly resist you as she creates her own identity.

Though it is natural for parents to resist such a development, it is a shift that is best for both parent and child. If, after all, the parent holds as one goal that her adolescent become an adult who can think for herself and make intelligent decisions for herself, then that adolescent must become capable of forming independent opinions for herself.

There will be, as I have noted, issues over which there will be no absolute winner, issues best resolved by negotiation. Reaching that point—recognizing that reality—can be difficult for both parent and adolescent.

The practice of agreeing to disagree evolves most smoothly and naturally if it starts in the earliest stages of latency, around the age of eight, and if it is applied to somewhat neutral areas. It might be applied, for example, to the choice of books. Let's say you loved *Alice in Wonderland,* but she can't get into it; she loves the Baby-Sitter Club series instead. Now, you could ridicule her books, point out that *Alice* is a classic, whereas Baby-Sitter is a soap opera. Or you could tell her you're delighted she's found books she really likes and that maybe someday she'll give *Alice* a second chance.

In the latter case, you are sending her the message that you and she may have different tastes when it comes to books, but you both love to read and you respect her choice. You are also telling her that you respect her. And that the two of you can differ in this regard, but nothing bad will happen to her.

The same message can also be conveyed rather painlessly over music and TV programs. "Okay, I admit it, your music doesn't appeal to me at all. But I think we can both live with that. After all, you don't like my classical music. . . . It's true, we both like the Beatles, and you even seem to like a bit of Elvis, Bob Dylan, and Ray Charles, so maybe there's hope for us yet."

In addition to teaching the principle of agreeing to disagree, you are in a subtle way teaching tolerance. As she gets older, she will be able to be tolerant of people who are different from her, of a different color, of a different religion. What you said to her about *Alice in Wonderland* or the music of Guns N' Roses applies again: "Just because Janey doesn't believe in Jesus and we do, that doesn't mean that you can't have her for a friend. She's a terrific girl."

There are of course countless homes in which the contrary message would be expressed, that indeed, you can't have Janey as a friend because her views are different. Not only does such a message instill intolerance and bigotry, it can be damaging to the child's development. It teaches her that she can't have an independent opinion, and that she can't accept people who hold different beliefs from her. The deeper message is that she can't accept the concept of agreeing to disagree.

A child raised in that environment will be stunted developmentally, and she might also be an extremely difficult adolescent to live with. She will have rejected the fundamental idea of agreeing to disagree, and that will include those areas where she and her parents disagree.

The issues between parent and adolescent grow increasingly more meaningful and emotionally loaded as the adolescent grows older. Now it is a matter of the choice not of books but of friends of the opposite sex, of sexual behavior, or perhaps, as we saw earlier in this chapter, of college.

Unless there is a foundation in place between parent and child, a principle that says, "We can differ, yet out of love and respect for each other we will find a way, a compromise," there will likely be the meanest and most damaging of battles in which no one ever wins.

LISTENING WITH RESPECT

The second element of negotiation, which like the first, will sound obvious, is listening to your child with respect.

In many ways, this is central to the whole possibility of negotiation. After all, why would your child be responsive to negotiation if he didn't feel that you took his communications seriously?

Developing that quiet trust takes time and ideally starts early, when the child first comes home from the playground or school with the most fantastic, garbled, breathless stories about what "he did and she did and I did." As wild as his tales may be, he needs your attention. If all he gets is a grunted "Good," he begins to get the idea that you are not really listening to him.

It is an idea that is nurtured every time he puts a question to his father that is greeted with an indifferent "I don't know, ask your mother." Or reinforced every time he puts forward some uncertain plan or request, and it is dismissed all too quickly without explanation or discussion.

Parents who treat their children that way do not understand that whatever the child's communications may be, however silly, they are important to the child. They deserve to be listened to, and they deserve a respectful response, even if it's a "No, I'm sorry, sweetie, but we can't have a butterfly farm in the living room."

Not listening with respect to your child is a form of ridicule, and it snowballs. By the time he is eleven or twelve, he has decided that what he says to his parents doesn't matter; they aren't listening. Then, instead of a negotiation based on the implicit idea that parents respect what their child has to say, you have warring sides. As soon as one side gets three words out, the other is yelling and screaming in opposition.

If the practice of listening with respect is not instilled early in the child's life, a parent may be able to repair the damage over time, much the way a stepparent creates trust. She works for two or three years building bridges.

When you stop to think about it, if you really value your child, there's nothing more important than listening to him.

GRADED NEGOTIATION AND GRADED RESPONSIBILITY

The third element, graded negotiation, is also rooted in early childhood and parenting.

Negotiation between a parent and an adolescent is going to be much easier if there is something of a natural pattern for it. This commonly means a relationship that in the beginning was completely one-sided. The parents were the authoritarians, setting limits and deciding what the child would be allowed to do and not do. As the child grew older, she argued for more privilege, more power, more independence. In this model, it was the parents who were able to dispense privilege, to give the child more and more of what she wanted. Or, by the time the child reached adolescence, to negotiate what she wanted.

Increasingly, in exchange for power, the parents extract a new kind of responsibility from the child. It might start with bedtime. She can stay up till 10:00, but she has to agree to be in bed by 9:30 and to read for half an hour. Perhaps she is next allowed to watch two more TV shows during the week, but in exchange she must clean her room every week.

By adolescence, the nature of the negotiation and its importance might escalate, but the process is the same. Yes, you may take the family car, but you have to be back by midnight, no matter how late the party goes on.

Or, let's say the family's plan to go away for a weekend conflicts with a big school event on Saturday night. She is only fourteen, but she insists that she can be left alone. Arbitrarily rejecting her arguments and pleas might leave you less anxious,

but it won't do much for your child's self-esteem or your relationship with her. Resolving this difficulty can build good feelings and trust on both sides. Perhaps you tell her that the whole
thing makes you nervous, especially the idea of her being home
alone. But if she can arrange a sleepover with a friend whose
parents will be home, and if she can be trusted to stick to your
usual rules on parties, you'll give it a shot. If anything goes
wrong, it will be a long, long time before she is trusted in this
manner again.

Families who approach negotiation in this graded manner
over the years slide quite naturally into adolescent negotiations of
the most difficult kind.

There is a real problem, however, for those families in which
the parents never set early, reasonable limits. If a child was allowed to do pretty much whatever she wanted, if her freedoms
were never negotiated, it is going to be extremely difficult for a
parent to try to start negotiating in adolescence.

From her perspective, there is no familiarity with this process,
nor is there anything for the parents to negotiate. After all, she
has always done whatever she pleased. No parent ever told her to
turn her lights out at 9:30; she stayed up as late as she desired.
Her television time was never monitored; she watched what she
wanted, when she wanted. To suddenly have restrictions placed
on her life in adolescence will seem unfair, completely arbitrary,
and authoritarian. And especially when she sees her friends being
granted more freedom and control over their lives. Large battles
seem inevitable.

To some degree, this problem can be avoided if parents begin
to assert themselves by early latency, when the child is around
seven years of age. Even then, there will be the established "anything goes" pattern to be broken. But the child's disposition at
that age to please her parents can help establish a new relationship, one that includes the setting of limits and the practice of
graded negotiation and graded responsibility.

There are some issues in every family that are nonnegotiable, or in my view ought to be. As I noted earlier, these would include anything that is dangerous to self and others. There is nothing to negotiate about drugs or casual sex or drinking and driving, or, in a quite different category, about certain family obligations. Cousin Sarah's wedding is a must, even if you always hated her. Aunt Ann's funeral is a must, even if you never liked her either. When Grandma comes to dinner, you must eat with us, and she will be invited to your graduation, like it or not.

Those are special categories and are best limited in number. In all other situations, as I said, to me the key to dealing with an adolescent lies in being able to negotiate, in being able to set intelligent and appropriate priorities to eliminate those issues not worth arguing over and then to negotiate the rest.

And if a pattern of graded negotiation and responsibility has been established over the years, if the parent has consistently listened with respect to the child over the years, and if both parent and adolescent have agreed that they can disagree yet remain respectful and loving—then the essential elements exist for them to negotiate and work through the toughest of adolescent problems.

9

Relinquishing Control

The preceding three chapters share a common thread: the idea of parents relinquishing control.

It is a critical development, certainly if one accepts the thesis that parents are caretakers of their children, with the responsibility of leading them toward an independent life, one in which they can think and act on their own and take care of themselves.

In other words, as the adolescent grows and changes, so does the role of the parents and, hopefully, the parents themselves.

Relinquishing control is not easy for a loving parent. In fact, it is a painful process, and it takes a very mature parent to do so, to be able to trust an adolescent on important issues. But, ultimately, if a parent is unable to relinquish control, it will be extremely difficult for the adolescent to mature, flourish, and become an adult.

Relinquishing control does not mean you should remove yourself from the adolescent's life. You are still very much present as model and guide, as a voice that causes him to think about his proposed actions, that causes him to rethink his stated plans.

But you are no longer the same arbiter of judgment you were, no longer the final censor.

Relinquishing control is not accomplished overnight or by declaration. It is best achieved as a gradual process throughout the high school years.

In talking with parents, I find it helps to think ahead to a time when their child has completed high school and become self-sufficient or is in college. By that point, it is generally agreed, they want to feel reasonably comfortable, trusting that their child can fairly well take care of himself, that he can and will use reasonably good judgment.

Obviously, this happy state does not automatically occur simply because the adolescent finishes high school and gets a job or packs up and goes off to college. This point of responsible young adulthood is the result of years of gradually increased independence and responsibility. It is the result of all the growing, struggling, searching, talking, and negotiating since the beginning of adolescence.

Back when your child was thirteen and announced that he wanted to go steady, you were able to deny him permission and tried to explain why going steady at thirteen would only limit his social possibilities and fun. He might not have accepted your views, but most likely he accepted your authority.

Asserting the same authority when he is fifteen is problematic, although you might be able to reason with him more effectively.

But by the age of nineteen, when he is away at college or has his own job or apartment, neither your authority nor your reasoning power is going to mean much. Then you are depending on his judgment, which, after all, you have helped to shape all through adolescence.

You can smooth this process by creating a transitional year from adolescence to young adulthood. You might well use the year from age seventeen to eighteen, commonly the last year of high school, as a time when you try to be as uncontrolling as possible, when you try to treat your child as a young adult, when you encourage him to be self-directing. This gives him the chance to practice being the independent soul he will actually be the next year when he is living away from home.

AVOIDING RADICAL SOLUTIONS

Lessening control at this time can also help you to avoid the damaging fallout from natural conflicts of this period.

We've already considered aspects of conflicts over role identity, when the adolescent reaches for the role she envisions for herself in society. As we saw, the choice of a college or a career can trigger terrible battles within a family. The outcome can be disastrous if parents don't ultimately concede the struggle, which is, at bottom, really a struggle over who controls the adolescent's life.

Let's assume the struggle is over a college choice, which also frequently implies a future role. Perhaps she says she wants to pursue what she has dreamed of ever since she was thirteen: she wants to be an actress. And you, while aware of her general interest in acting, never realized how serious it was. Even so, being an actress strikes you as a fantasy that should have been abandoned long ago. You would like to see her become a lawyer.

If you try to prevail by power, you run the risk of inadvertently forcing a radical solution to the problem.

Perhaps you will cause her to act radically. "Fine," she announces. "I'm going off to New York where I'll work as a waitress and put myself through acting school. The hell with you. I'm going to live my own life."

Or maybe you'll be able to force her to capitulate to your views, but in the process she may bury a lot of anger, at least temporarily, and harbor considerable resentment. Remember the medical school students I mentioned who have come to me saying, "I hate this place. Becoming a doctor was never my idea in the first place."

Either way, her radically negative or radically passive solution can lead to great unhappiness later in life.

Instead, if you recognize that this is a possible outcome and that this is a time when control should be lifted, you can create fruitful discussion and compromise. Maybe that means saying, "Well, we certainly disagree about this. But you're still my daughter and I love you. So I'm willing to give it a try. What about this as a compromise? Apply to the various colleges you've been talking about. And then, when you're accepted to one you like, tell the school you want to defer for a year. Practically every college in America allows that today. Then try acting school for a year, and we both can see what we're really talking about. If it works out, fine, we can take it from there. If not, as one alternative, you have the college."

I think it's preferable to end up with parents who are not completely satisfied, whose children may not be completely what they wanted them to be. More important, their children will be independent, relatively happy young adults, pursuing goals in a positive, thoughtful way because their parents have helped them to think hard about their life choices.

INTRANSIGENCE OVER TOUGH ISSUES

The issue of relinquishing control is also frequently enmeshed in choices of boyfriends and girlfriends. Let's say your adolescent daughter starts dating one young man regularly, and there is a difference in religion, which is a matter of great importance in your family. Or a difference in race, which remains a widespread barrier in our society. Or maybe the problem is that you simply don't like the young man; he isn't bright enough or ambitious enough in your view. A professional colleague of mine was beside himself when his daughter became smitten with a young man who worked in a gas station near their country weekend place.

I mentioned the thirteen-year-old who wants to go steady but bows to your authority. If he doesn't, you can easily fall into a power struggle with him, which will probably cause him to feel even stronger about his steady relationship. But if you can restrain yourself to comments about the disadvantages of going steady at that age, chances are that this early infatuation will fade in a relatively short time.

Summer romances are also short-lived, almost by definition. They can be intense, but they are limited to the summer, a condition the involved adolescents are unconsciously aware of: they know that these are "safe" relationships, that they will end come September when it is time to return to the real world.

If a disturbing relationship occurs when your child is sixteen or seventeen, your prohibiting it will most likely only drive it underground, and with greater passion and intensity. If it occurs later, when your child is at college, your opposition will necessarily be somewhat removed, probably long-distance, and of little impact. (There is one exception, economic control, which I'll consider shortly.)

So you are faced with a fairly clear choice. You can prohibit, banish, and rant and rave, which will push matters underground, and drop a certain amount of poison into your relationship with your child, or you can start to relinquish control.

The real challenge for you is not the worrisome, maybe horrifying romance your child flaunts in your face—which, chances are, will run its course fairly quickly if left alone—but whether you can follow your head instead of your heart. Can you say: "If you want to see John, okay, you're old enough to decide that for yourself. But I want to be honest with you . . ."?

If not, what usually happens is an escalation into war, the

kind of explosiveness that ends up with a family in my office, in which the parents have won some kind of victory, but I'm not sure what it is. They have an unhappy, bitter, perhaps depressed, dissatisfied child in their home, and life is terribly unpleasant for everyone.

A number of these issues are dealt with in the movie *Dirty Dancing,* mentioned earlier, which provides insight into adolescent fantasy and sexual identity. The film is also an interesting exploration of the relationship between an adolescent girl and her father, and the testing of love, trust, and flexibility between them.

Set in a summer resort hotel, *Dirty Dancing* focuses on the explorations of an upper-middle-class girl, the darling of her doctor father who still calls her "Baby," though she is seventeen and about to enter college. Baby becomes infatuated with the resort's dance instructor, something of a drifter and gigolo from a family of blue-collar house painters. But it is the girl, making independent decisions and becoming sexually active, who seduces the stud.

Along the way, she befriends his dancing partner, who has become pregnant by one of the hotel's waiters, a young medical school student. In her effort to help this woman, Baby turns to her father, and we see the depth of their relationship.

First, she goes to him to borrow $250 for an abortion but says she cannot tell him what the money is for. It is a moment with which any parent can empathize. He asks her if she is in trouble. "You always said you could tell me anything," he reminds her, a statement that reveals the closeness and openness they shared. But this is one time when he simply has to trust her, she pleads, and he agrees.

Later, she turns to him again, when the abortion is botched and the woman lies bleeding in her cabin. Now her father responds as both father and doctor, and in the middle of the night, he treats the woman.

In return, he asks his daughter to keep away from "those

people." As the movie unfolds, she does not, nor does he try to restrict her or burden his wife with the disturbing events. In a moving confrontation between daughter and father, she does not apologize for acting in her independent way, but she reminds him of her love. Despite everything, she says, "I'm in this family too, and you can't keep giving me the silent treatment."

There is, of course, a happy ending in which the father realizes that he was wrong in his opinion of the dance instructor, whom he had accused of making his dancing partner pregnant, abandoning her, and taking up with his innocent daughter. He learns that it was the medical student—of all people and models—who was the villain, and he apologizes to the dance instructor in front of his daughter. "When I'm wrong, I say I'm wrong," he tells the fellow, as his daughter beams with pride and love.

She meanwhile has learned a lot about dancing and apparently a lot about making love, but we are left with the feeling that the summer romance is over. She has another life to lead, starting with Mt. Holyoke College in a few weeks.

The father's willingness to trust his daughter, to relinquish control and take a great risk, was difficult, painful, and yet ultimately rewarding. Through it all, though disapproving, he never rejected her, and she remained a loving daughter and very much a part of the family. She did not run off with the young man, as one could imagine her doing if her father had been obstinate and ordered her to stop seeing the fellow. But as tough as it was, the father was able to understand that his daughter, about to enter college, was at the point in adolescence and life where she must be allowed independence, even while he made known to her his serious concerns.

It doesn't always work this way. These are issues that strain the closest of families. I have seen cases of this sort where the parents are unable to win their child over to their position and cannot bring themselves to trust their child further. In desperation, they then use their ultimate weapon, economic control, threatening to cut the child off without financial support or tuition if she doesn't do as they say. But as I noted earlier, that is a weapon no one survives. The child may temporarily succumb to her parents, but her bitterness and anger are so intense and deep, the family is essentially ruptured. The chances are good that the child will turn her back on her parents and go out on her own.

Where there is intransigence, everybody loses, and it is the parent who I assume will be the mature agent in an explosive dispute. It is the parent who, at some point, must step back as Baby's father did in *Dirty Dancing* and ask himself: "Do I want to lose my child, or can I repair our relationship?" It is the parent who must recognize that if the war continues, he is going to lose his child emotionally and perhaps physically as well. It is the parent who has to ask if there is instead some way to rescue this situation, some way to put respect and love back into the relationship, some way to get to the peace table.

I have seen a similar dilemma for parents of gay and lesbian adolescents who send word from college that they have discovered their real sexuality. After the initial shock, the parents have to decide whether to accept their child or not. They have to decide what their child is worth to them. Undoubtedly, we all have seen families where there is no reconciliation. The gay son or lesbian daughter is banished from the family.

With a different kind of intransigence, I tried to help one orthodox Jewish family in which the parents decided that their son, who had married a Catholic woman, had, in effect, died. Both the son and his bride were psychiatric students whom I knew, lovely people. But his parents would not consider a reconciliation. They actually sat "shivah" for him, said the prayers for the dead for him.

There is yet another fairly common form of intransigence. Under the guise of parental love and pride, the parent takes the position that there really isn't anyone good enough for his or her son or daughter.

In reality, this parent is overly attached to the child and incapable of accepting anyone the child connects with. This parent will not relinquish any control at all.

And that is what we come back to, the ability of parents to relinquish control, to face and live with the inevitable. When does the parent finally recognize that a particular relationship, choice of job, of lifestyle, as contrary as it may seem, as unwise as it may seem, is still a function of the child's life? When does the parent start to see the adolescent as an adult, albeit a young adult?

The legal age is eighteen. But the psychological age is another matter.

In my experience, adulthood comes not when the child declares, "I don't want you to tell me what to do anymore," but rather when the parent begins to sense a new quality. Often it comes in the child's early twenties, when the parent gets the feeling that "my child really seems to know what he's doing, really seems to know where he's going."

At that point, hopefully, the relationship within the family is such that he can say to his parents, "This is what I'm planing to do . . . ," and they can feel free to say to him: "We have a question about that. Let us tell you what it is. . . . If you really want to pursue that, we'll help you. But give some thought to these few points. . . ."

That's something of an ideal relationship. Early in his twenties, when his adult life is really being launched, he brings his plans home, not because he requires parental approval to proceed, but because he respects and loves his parents, as they do him, and together they are capable of discussing such serious issues, listening with great respect to what the others have to say, with no one insisting on his own way.

When that occurs, control truly has been relinquished by the parents, and in its place is loving collaboration, a quality that can sustain their relationship for a lifetime.

10

Role Identity and Parental Frustrations

We have been exploring the balance of power between parents and adolescents, and how it evolves. Nowhere is this more clearly demonstrated than in the issues that arise over the search for role identity in late adolescence.

This stage is defined by Erik Erikson as the time when the adolescent tries to affirm his or her role in society, a role that is self-sustaining and to some extent family-sustaining.

Affirming her role is her declaration of adulthood: "This is what I want to be. . . . This is how I want to live. . . ." And to realize these goals, she must take a number of steps that are critical to the formation of the adult life: selecting a meaningful job, choosing a college, deciding on a particular career, selecting a mate.

In a sense, there is awareness of role identity in early childhood when three- and four-year-olds play at being various types of people whom they see as important in society. They are policemen and firefighters; they are mommies and daddies. The roles they identify with change as they move through midchildhood into latency and learn about an increasing number of possibilities.

The more serious work of defining a realistic role identity begins around the middle of the high school years. For those who do not intend to go to college, it's a time of deciding on work after high school. At one time, this meant choosing a form of apprenticeship. Though those days are largely over, a young person might still decide to be a garage mechanic, or a hairdresser, or perhaps a travel agent—all jobs that might involve courses as well as on-the-job training.

For others, ideas begin to take shape in high school, but the execution is delayed, increasingly so in our culture. There is college, and frequently graduate school. Many graduate schools of business will accept only candidates who have two or three years of employment experience. In medicine, after four years of medical school, there is now a period of specialization, three more years to become a pediatrician, for example, or at least five years to become a child psychiatrist.

This state of affairs alters the nature of adolescence. Until an adolescent passes through the stage of role identity, that individual is not an adult. The educational process in our culture lengthens the time that the adolescent is dependent on his family, delaying adulthood and, in many cases, creating a problem for everyone.

At one time in our culture, or even today in more primitive cultures, the three phases of adolescence were compressed, that is to say, between the ages of about twelve and fifteen the adolescent established his own identity, affirmed his sexual identity, and determined his role identity. At that point, he moved into the adult world, became a hunter, a farmer, took a mate, and began to reproduce.

But with the artificial extension of adolescence through various types and years of graduate schools, we have delayed the point of true independence from the family, the point of real adult existence. In our society, until you are earning a living and self-sufficient, you are not a true adult.

The strain is felt by adolescents and their families, and much more so in recent years. The economy has not allowed adolescents to find suitable jobs, even after all those years of schooling, and they are thrown back upon their families, sometimes for years, now as split characters—part adolescent, part adult—a dilemma we will explore in chapter 14.

THE LIMITS
OF PARENTAL INFLUENCE

Among loving parents, there is a natural instinct to want to directly influence, if not to completely shape and manage, the process of role identity. But there are healthy limits to how well that works.

Essentially, the adolescent is going through an internal search, feeling out and examining real and imagined possibilities.

Parents can enrich a child's education and try to expose him to a variety of role possibilities. And parents can be the most meaningful models.

You want your child to become a lawyer like you? Or take over the family business from you? Be a good model.

If following in your footsteps means coming home at nine every night, working through every vacation, and not having enough time for your son, don't be surprised if he turns in another direction when he chooses his own field.

I tell my doctor friends who want desperately for their children to go into medicine: "Don't push it. Your children have seen enough medicine for them to decide for themselves. Be a good doctor, let them see that you're doing work that matters to you, let them see that you care about people, and be a good father or mother." In my experience, when the pressure is removed and the choice is left to the child, the child ends up in medical school.

I have also seen countless cases in which the child had a need to reject the parental model for a period of time. They major in fields like medieval philosophy and drift for a few years, perhaps working in a job that is light-years from the parental model, and just as far from their own true interests. Then, having shown themselves that they are independent, they take a fresh look at their career choice. Being a lawyer or doctor or whatever isn't such a bad idea after all, they are finally able to say. And they head for the nearest appropriate graduate school. They are a few years behind, but without making the decision in their own way, at their own pace, they wouldn't have made it at all.

There is also the matter of timing. This is the worst possible time to pressure an adolescent into a particular field. Ideally, when the child is wrestling in a serious fashion with the issue of what he is going to be, the parents should be relinquishing control. By this point, the adolescent is usually well into his struggle for independence and most likely to resent and resist such interference with his life. Pressure at this time is likely to fuel rebelliousness.

I've seen relationships poisoned when parents nag their children, who have just started college, over the choice of a major and a career. Only a small percentage of college freshman have an idea of where they are headed. The rest are struggling with the anxieties of the new world they have entered; for most, this is their first experience living away from home without supervision. It is generally not until the third year of college that students turn seriously to the issues and decisions of role identity.

Even then, while parents can certainly discuss possibilities with their student-child and make their views known, the child should be allowed to explore and blossom as much as possible. Some parents may decide that this means supporting him financially through graduate school.

Parents can sometimes influence decisions by drawing on experience and being dispassionate, letting the evidence speak for itself. After all, you have lived in the real world a good deal longer that your son or daughter. Your child's view of a particular field might be quite romantic.

One father I know had a number of reservations about his daughter's leanings toward advertising. He told her the decision was up to her, but she should understand that advertising, in his experience, breeds great unhappiness. It is essentially a business of cleverness and camouflage. At times, it is a craft of deception. Would she be happy spending years writing about the glories of toilet paper? True, there are glamorous offices and good money, but try to look deeper, he urged her. He also arranged a lunch for her with a friend of his whom she knew and liked, who had been quite successful in advertising but had great reservations about recommending it as a career.

The girl soon changed her mind. Interestingly, her father thought that if she had tried it, she would have become disillusioned fairly quickly and changed fields. In other words, she would not have stubbornly wasted years and years. His efforts saved her a certain amount of time.

I think there are lessons to be learned here.

First of all, if your child chooses a career that leaves you worried, where is it written that you are always right? If you are faced with such a situation, think about it hard and long, alone and with her.

Then, if you are still convinced of your wisdom and her choice still leaves you worried, bear in mind that the chances are good that she will change careers if she discovers for herself that the choice was indeed a mistake. In many cases, only by making the discovery herself will she accept it. As a loving parent, you want to spare her all pain. But that is not always possible or even always best in the end.

Of course, there can be great disappointments over a child's choice. In one family with four children, where both parents were professionals, two of the children became doctors, another, a lawyer, and the fourth, a ski instructor.

That was what she wanted to do, the fourth child announced, after completing one of the most highly regarded colleges in America. It was a form of rebellion, the parents decided, and they went along with it, as disappointed as they were. They hoped and expected she would pass through what they saw as a phase, but she did not. She married another ski instructor, who was a farmer as well, and together they sank roots in northern New England, teaching on the mountain in the winter and farming the rest of the year, a life they both loved. With two children of her own in the local schools, she became involved in the school system and recently went back to graduate school for a degree in education.

This new career choice pleased her parents, but I think they had long ago accepted the course and life their daughter had chosen. They liked their son-in-law and loved their grandchildren. They overcame their initial shock and disappointment, which might well have separated them, and were able to keep their child a loving daughter.

NEGATIVE INFLUENCE

Not all efforts by parents to control their children are clear and conscious.

I think of a friend of mine who has been quite successful in the real estate business. His passion in life is painting, and he is extremely good at it. As far back as he can recall, he loved to paint and early in childhood declared his intention to become a painter. His parents, however, dismissed the idea. They did not argue with him about it, or threaten him, but it was always made clear to him that no one could make a living as a painter. Painting would be fine as a hobby, they maintained, but it was silly to think of it otherwise. From the way my friend described this experience to me, I concluded that his parents were unaware of

how they denigrated and ridiculed his dream. But they beat it out
of him.

I have heard of other parents who used guilt in a similar manner. Being an actor, they told their son, was for people who really
couldn't do anything else, and who didn't want to do anything
else. The implication was that actors were inferior people.

It takes quite an effort for children to overcome such parental
scorn and assert themselves. I have seen it happen, students dropping out of college and graduate school, finally coming to grips
with the idea that their life has been determined by their parents,
finally asking themselves, "Is my role in life doing what my
parents tell me to do?"

Parents can also have a negative influence on their children by
removing themselves altogether from the role-identity process. In
the cases I've seen, the parents were highly successful and provided for their children's material needs, paid for good private
schools, gave them more than adequate allowances, but they were
emotionally distant from their children.

As a result, these children experienced life as if they were
unwanted. When it came to role identity, they were overwhelmed. On the one hand, they received no stimulation or
guidance from their parents. On the other, they saw the achievements of their parents and felt that their own situation was
somewhat hopeless. They didn't feel they could exceed their parents, which is often one of the unconscious motivations in the
process of selecting a role.

This is a dangerous combination, the lack of stimulus, the
overwhelming achievements of their parents, plus the general
feeling that nobody cares anyway. I have seen it lead to severe
psychological problems in adolescents, a turmoil that blocks these
young adults from ever growing up. They can't find their role;
they can't find themselves.

We have all seen grown people like this who seem to spend

their entire life in a search for identity, trying out roles, leading lives without focus.

PROTECTING YOUR CHILD

In contrast to the neglecting parent is the overattached parent, which in my experience is the more common phenomenon.

Studies show that with infants, parents can inflict psychological damage if they are abusive or neglectful as well as if they are suffocating in their caring. Leonard Shengold, in his book *Soul Murder,* uses the wonderful terms "not-enoughness" and "too-muchness" to express the contrasting conditions that can severely damage children.

With adolescents, especially around the issue of role identity, I find a common tendency among parents toward overprotectiveness. In chapter 1, I noted that the word *adolescent* comes from the Latin *adolescere,* which means "to grow up." Indeed, throughout this book, we have been exploring the ways that parents can keep that definition and that reality in mind. And in this chapter, I have made the case that attempting to exert too much influence in the choice of role can be damaging to both parent and adolescent. The parent may very well have an unconscious agenda to control and suppress the child, who senses this and ends up rejecting or resenting the parent.

Let me extend that idea. Adolescents cannot be protected from the demands of life and society. There's a limit to how much parents can do, and probably should do, to shield their adolescent from the blows of society.

In my practice I've recently seen several adolescents in their twenties, who were brought in by their parents. All these young adults, their parents told me, were depressed. More accurately, they were generally unhappy and slightly depressed, which is much milder than clinical depression. They had the same prob-

lem: unemployment. Each of these adolescents had finished college and could not, a year later, eighteen months later, find a
suitable job. There was no way their parents could protect them
from an economy that was in a recession.

The outbreak of war can be another severe blow. The adolescent studying to become a great architect may be told to forget
school, to put on a uniform and learn how to shoot a rifle. A
parent cannot prevent that war.

As of this writing, it appears that the whole practice of medicine in America is going to be radically changed. Between man-
aged care and President Clinton's health-care proposals, a medical
school student is confronted with enormous uncertainty.

There is nothing any parent can do to alter the ways society
impinges. Cultures change and the results are disruptive. All a
parent can do in the face of such profound shifts is to be supportive and offer help.

Overprotectiveness can also be a tool in a parent's unconscious
campaign to control an adolescent. In that case, the motivation is
not so much to shield the child as it is to suppress the child.

For both parent and adolescent, the final stages of role definition and selection are going to be smoother and healthier if
parents can be aware of their own tendencies toward overprotection.

In the actual parting, the creation of the so-called empty
nest, I find that most parents are ambivalent about this mile-
stone.

There is the common wisdom that parents are bereft, almost
mourning the loss of their children. They can't stand the silence
that suddenly falls over their homes.

I think there is some sense of loss, to be sure. The separation
can be painful. It can also signal an unwelcome change of life, of
growing older. But in my experience most parents also welcome

the change. They are relieved of the daily burden of physically and psychologically caring for their vulnerable adolescent.

Not that the caring ceases. We are not like animals who can easily separate from their young. Our caring is never ending, even when our children are long past adolescence, even when they have families of their own. A parent is a parent forever, and that does not imply overprotectiveness.

Unlike animals, we have a sense of the future. Our thoughts of our children become enmeshed in the future. Will they finally, after all our discussions and after all their yearnings, land a job that appeals to them? Will they succeed in their chosen field? Will they marry well, be happy? Will they finally settle into the role they have chosen for themselves with some measure of comfort and satisfaction?

These are transcendent and universal concerns etched eternally in the minds of parents everywhere who love their children. Freud was absolutely right when he said that the toughest of all jobs is being a parent.

11

Divorce: Complex Trauma, but Manageable

I have the impression that most people, certainly couples considering it, think that divorce is not so damaging to adolescents.

Painful perhaps, as divorce is to everyone touched by it, but not the bewildering explosion it is to, say, a six-year-old who suddenly feels as if half his world has been blown away. An adolescent, according to this view, has enough maturity and perspective to absorb the rupture and adjust to a new style of life at home without serious scarring.

But divorce can be a devastating event in the life of an adolescent, depending on how parents manage it.

To begin with, there is the profound emotional blow of seeing the dissolution of his parents' marriage and his family as he has known it for fifteen or sixteen years. During all those years, most likely, his parents presented their marriage to him as terrific, full of love and joy. Suddenly, it has all come apart. Does this mean that for all those years, his parents—the two people he trusted more than anyone else in the world—were deceiving him? Lying to him?

Even if there were signs of trouble, chances are he denied

them, denial being such a strong and useful defense. Adolescents who have come to me for treatment because of problems stemming from a recent divorce between their parents invariably start out exclaiming their total surprise. "I never guessed this could have happened," they say. And then, maybe three months into therapy, they start talking about how their father stopped coming home every night, or the fights their parents had, or how they stopped sleeping in the same room. But when it was happening, the meaning of these clues was more than they could rationally absorb. So they denied it.

The blow of divorce is not diminished by the fact that the adolescent has been struggling against these same parents in his effort to separate and find his own identity. During that search, he remained emotionally and intellectually a part of his family.

Even though during that time he might begin to see his parents as less than perfect—people with dreadful taste in music and paleolithic political views who set moronic rules of behavior for him—paradoxically, he views their marriage as ideal.

That view of his parents' marriage is consistent with a pervasive quality of adolescence noted earlier in the book: it is a time of burning idealism. Applied to their own relationships, this idealism means finding the perfect mate, imagining the perfect marriage. They will love their partner forever, being loyal and faithful to this person forever. Romeo and Juliet, with all their defiant, doomed passion, are adolescent models.

Marriage is the institution that society and his parents upheld as something close to sacred. Certainly it was the container of his fantasies, a transcendent and stable element in his life.

From that perspective, one can begin to understand how the disillusionment that the idealistic adolescent feels over the divorce is numbing, wrapped in a profound loss of trust and faith.

OEDIPAL CONFUSION

A divorce in a family with adolescents is often a reflection of a midlife crisis, frequently on the part of the father. If that's the case, and he announces that he's leaving for a woman, say, in her twenties, the blow to his adolescent son is complicated by the fact that he himself is attracted to young women in their twenties. Among adolescents I have treated who faced such a development, their shared response was complete denial. They could not accept the fact that their father had done what he had done.

There is a different kind of emotional jolt for an adolescent girl when her father leaves her mother for a woman who is not that much older than herself. In Freudian terms, the disturbing issue of the incestuous sexual attraction that the adolescent unconsciously has felt for her father is raised by his actions. After all, he is actually having sex with a woman who is almost her age.

Judith Wallerstein, who has done significant recent studies on the effects of divorce on adolescents, raises questions about how it can color their later relationships much more than a divorce impinging on a younger child would.

A girl's first relationship with a male normally is with her father. She practices her first male-female relationships with her father, she practices being a woman with her father. This might take the form of an impromptu fashion show in which she models for him her new back-to-school clothes. Or it might take the form of a major argument with him over the environment, which is connected in part to her need to show herself that she can make points against male competition.

Stripped of her father, stripped of the first man in whom she invested her emotions, her love, it would not be surprising if she lost trust in such relationships. Nor would it be surprising if she became increasingly uncomfortable, uncertain of herself in relationships.

The young male adolescent loses his primary male model, the figure on whom he shaped himself and against whom he struggled. If it is the mother who triggers the divorce in order to live with another man, the male adolescent is vulnerable to severe Oedipal trauma and confusion.

It is not clear who suffers from a divorce more, the female or the male adolescent. For both, if the divorce of their parents is cloaked with sexual elements, the devastation will most likely be even greater than if the parents' explanation is free of sexual complications—a declaration that their love has faded or that they have decided they want to live different lives.

Beyond the Oedipal reverberations, the adolescents must face the fact that their parents are sexual creatures. Children, even as adults, don't normally think of their parents as actually having sex. That ideal marriage of their parents is asexual in the minds of adolescents, which makes it easier to idealize it. But if the divorce flags the reality of sex, as it certainly would when one or the other parent says, I'm leaving for a woman, or a man, the confusion is enormous and deeply upsetting for an adolescent who is in the process of trying to come to grips with his or her own sexual psychology.

Wallerstein's studies raise questions of how such traumatic losses might affect adolescents for years afterward in their efforts at establishing intimate relationships of their own. They are questions requiring more research, but which suggest disturbing conclusions.

Reading hundreds of applications to NYU Medical School every year, I frequently encounter yet another effect of divorce. "My parents went through a very bad divorce during my sophomore year" is the typical statement. "I was very upset by it, and my grades suffered that year."

Adolescents still need their family support systems. They are still, even in college, dependent on their parents in many ways, including for encouragement. During those tough college years, they need their parents to stand behind them if, say, their grades start to slide, and to provide a cheer when a big test is nailed, when a promotion comes on the college paper. They need to be able to reach out and have parents respond, "Yes, we'll send you an extra $100 for a ski trip."

When all of that crashes down, when the student goes home at Thanksgiving and finds his mother in tears, it is not uncommon for an entire academic year to be lost.

THE ADOLESCENT RESPONSE

Divorce strikes the adolescent differently from the young child. The six-year-old is going to color it with his magical powers. "I caused this. Somehow, in my little world, I had to have something to do with this. But I can also fix it."

The adolescent, on the other hand, tends to wonder, "What could I have done differently that would have held this marriage together?" He does not imagine that he was the single cause of the divorce, nor that he can magically bring his parents back together, but he feels a tinge of guilt. "I wish I hadn't been so demanding. They were always fighting over money, but I wanted to go to an expensive private school."

Often the adolescent feels that he can help by being an intermediary. He can go between his parents and the lawyers, and especially between the parents themselves. This kind of effort can become a damaging trap for the adolescent, as one parent, then the other, tries to enlist him on their side.

I treated one poor girl of fourteen whose life had become that of a messenger. Her parents were divorcing in a most bitter way, and neither would move out of the family house. The father claimed that he had paid for it, the mother that she had designed and furnished it. Neither would talk directly to the other, so the girl was enlisted as a messenger, going from the upstairs where the father lived to the main floor, where the mother lived, and back again, endlessly.

The girl's own regular life was shattered. Depressed, distraught, she became anorexic, which essentially was her way of protesting her treatment. Working with her, I got her to stop being a messenger. More or less, I got her parents to understand that they were abusing their child, and, that, whatever else they did in their divorce tactics, they had to permit her to resume her normal life.

With another similar case, the adolescent was older, close to graduating from high school. She felt a strong need to be around her parents all the time because she felt she was their only channel of communication. But playing that role was so depressing for her that she came to realize she could not continue. This was another of those power struggles in which neither mother nor father would leave the house. But once the girl wiped her hands of the mess, I was able to help the mother realize that her daughter actually had been enslaved and now had to be given back her life. Before long, the mother moved out of the house, and the girl got a place of her own.

THREE KINDS OF DIVORCE

Such hideous divorces, obviously, will take the greatest toll on the adolescent survivors.

It needn't be that way. As angry as husband and wife might be with each other, they can still think of their children.

The best divorces from my perspective are ones in which the parents come to me (or some other professional) for guidance before they have announced their plans to their children. Then, depending on the circumstances, we can sketch out a plan that will be least damaging for the children.

To start with, we can agree on the best way to break the news to the children, which is usually along the following lines: "This will come as something of a surprise to you, we know, but we have decided that it would be better for us and for you, for all of us, if we separate. You have undoubtedly felt lately that we have been having problems, lots of problems, that we're not getting on very well. And the truth is, we're not. The truth is, we are no longer in love and we think it would be better for everyone if we separated. The problem is between us. Please try to understand that. It has nothing to do with you or anything you've done. We both love you as much as ever, more than ever, but we have thought about this a lot now, talked it over a lot, and we are both convinced that we have to change our lives."

Part of the plan usually includes an agreement on who lives where, and that usually means that the husband moves out. It's best if he has a new place lined up when the announcement is made to the children, and he can move to it immediately. If he lingers, his presence will only confuse them and perhaps start them thinking that they can change the sad plan.

In the best of divorces, there are reasonable custody arrangements, assuring the children they will have regular access to their departing father.

Adolescents should be part of the planning of such arrangements. They are certainly capable of contributing, and it is their lives that are being reshaped. Being allowed to participate eases the feelings that they were to blame for the divorce. And where their suggestions are respected, their self-esteem is lifted. This is especially so where there is flexibility between the parents, a willingness to bend to the adolescent's needs. So perhaps there won't be a mandated visitation on Saturday nights, which is when the adolescent is most likely to have a date or want to be with friends.

Some couples do come to me in that early stage when damage can be minimized, but more often I see divorced families too long after the fact, when one of the children is responding to the divorce by behaving badly in school, or being truant, or being increasingly difficult at home.

Still, a troubled family that seeks professional guidance for those problems is better than one that does nothing. Adolescents over the age of twelve are quite capable of responding to family therapy. They can interrelate to the others in the family in the special atmosphere of the therapist's office, frequently with surprisingly good results in a rather short time. Six months is about average, with once-a-week sessions for the first three months, tapering off to once every two weeks and then once a month.

The third and worst kind of divorce reflects the obsessions and neurotic problems of the parents. These are typically divorces in which no one will move out of the family home, where in fact almost nothing can be agreed upon. Over months and even years, these wars continue, often because the parents are working out their anger at each other, or because one of them can't accept that the relationship is over.

These are the divorces that whiplash the children. They are imprisoned as intermediaries, manipulated by one parent, then the other. They are frequently hostage to alimony: no visits allowed to Dad unless he agrees to more alimony, a common tool of lawyers who have no idea of the damage they are wreaking on the affected children.

What is even better than an early consultation with a professional to ease the divorce blow is a genuine effort by the couple to save their marriage.

Yes, I am always pleased to counsel a couple set on divorce about ways to handle it that will be best for the children. But over the years, I have become somewhat cynical when couples protest their love of and concern for their children, especially when they have not made any real effort to save their marriage. What their children really need is an intact and functioning family, with supportive and loving parents. For all their guilt, the parents apparently haven't decided that their children are important enough for them to save their relationship and their family.

Quite simply, quite sadly, I am amazed at how few couples try to save their marriages.

AFTER THE BREAK

Young adolescents tend to want to live with the parent of the same sex, in part in the belief that this is the parent who is best going to understand the complicated changes the adolescent is experiencing.

Since most of the relocating parents are husbands, that means adolescent boys moving in with their fathers. In my experience, this is a step that usually unravels.

The adolescent makes the move with a number of fantasies in mind. Now that he and his father are together, out from under his mother, he imagines the rules will change. He will be a lot freer, suffer fewer restrictions in his social life, soon have his own car. His father, after all, has been through what he is going through and understands him so much better.

But rather than a closer bind and a collaborating parent, what the adolescent frequently encounters is a father who is preoccupied with his own new life. He has a new woman in his life, perhaps a whole new family. And while the adolescent son is welcomed, his fantasies are popped, and after a year or so, he decides that life back with Mom is better after all.

Which parent the adolescent chooses to live with is not nearly so important as his having both parents available to him and remaining a supportive part of his life.

Even when one parent moves to another city, as a change in life with a new job might well require, regular phone calls, regular visits, vacations spent together are all terribly important.

The absent parent's support for the custodial parent, especially in the area of discipline, is also vital. I always counsel
separating or divorced couples that they should present a united
front in matters of discipline. One can disagree with the other yet
still be supportive, and then separately, in a private conversation,
they can review their differences.

The son who has been docked a week's allowance because he
smoked in his room will be on the phone to his father, pleading
his case. Even if the father thinks the penalty is too stiff, he
should uphold it. "You disobeyed your mother and broke a house
rule. That doesn't go. She's right." That night, he can have a
separate conversation with her, raising the question of whether a
whole week's allowance may be too much.

Otherwise, there will be chaos at home, and the adolescent
will win a battle but lose a war. He will feel that he is able to defy
his mother's rules, but he will also feel that he has even less of a
sturdy home foundation than ever.

If the divorced parents can provide consistency and discipline
to the shattered family, the damage of divorce may well be
diminished.

Such cooperation can also make life somewhat easier for the
single parent, who is usually the mother. (The Census Bureau
reported that in 1992 fathers headed 14 percent of single-parent
homes, which was up from 10 percent in 1980, but still a small
percentage of the total.) Not surprisingly, one of her most difficult new roles is that of disciplinarian. Traditionally, that is a role
of the father, and though marriages are changing and responsibilities within families are as well, the mother is still the more
comforting and sheltering of the two. "Just wait till your father
gets home" is still the common threat. Children still grow up
more in fear of their fathers, in this context, than their mothers.

It is, then, a very difficult leap for the mother to fill both
roles, to be the warm, affectionate primary caregiver and the
disciplinarian as well. This is especially so, it seems, for mothers

with adolescent sons. And it is with that situation that the non-custodial father's support of her is most critical.

This is not to suggest that the reverse is not true. In the minority of cases where the father becomes the custodial parent, the adolescent still needs the continued attention and love of the mother, and the father needs her backing when it comes to discipline.

STEPPARENTS AND BLENDED FAMILIES

Becoming a stepparent to an adolescent requires patience and diplomacy. Let's consider what the stepfather of an adolescent girl, for example, is up against.

Typically, the adolescent has just had her own churning life, already so complex and clouded by the very nature of adolescence, further disturbed by the divorce. She has suffered all the blows described in this chapter. She has forged a new relationship with her mother and is wrestling with her conflicted feelings about her father, her anger with him, her need for him.

And into this picture steps her mother's new husband. Immediately, she resents him for taking time and emotional energy away from her mother. Additionally, she is probably confused and troubled by the idea that this new man is sleeping with her mother.

In a broad sense, this intruder has no credentials, no right to expect that the adolescent will automatically respect him, never mind automatically love him. The intruder will be wise to tread lightly and carefully. He should not expect to be accepted as a real parent or even called "Dad." In fact, to defuse that potential issue, he might suggest that his new stepdaughter call him by his first name.

He should expect to be tested by her, and probably for the

first two years of this new relationship, he should leave all matters of discipline to his new wife and her ex-husband.

If the intruder brings a child or children of his own with him, life can be even more difficult and complicated. Now it is not only one adolescent and two adults adjusting to one another but several relationships being balanced. The newly married adults are learning to live with each other, which can be difficult enough without any children. The children are getting accustomed to a new parent plus new "brothers" and "sisters."

Don't expect the children to behave like siblings when they aren't. I have heard of great strains among the children, but there can also be happy relationships created by these mergers: a young boy, for example, finally acquires the big brother he always wanted.

There can be quite unexpected results as well. One newly married couple came to me quite distressed. They had stumbled upon the teenage son from one family heavily petting with the teenage daughter from the other. This was not incipient incest, since the adolescents had no biological sibling relationship. But it was very disturbing nonetheless. If it had been the adolescent boy and, say, the girl next door, the parents might have cautioned them, or bawled them out, and gone about their lives. This situation, however, was obviously different.

We agreed that it would be best to treat it like a dating relationship that had to be carefully supervised. It would make sense to caution the two, remind them that they were, after all, living under the same roof. But allow them to date if they wanted.

For some time in this new blended family situation, discipline should be the domain of the natural parent, at least until both parents agree to a set of rules and until each has developed the kind of relationship in which the other's children will accept discipline from them. Indeed, it might not be so easy for the adults to reach this point. They might have truly different views on discipline, an area that wasn't much explored before they married each other.

The dynamics of the blended family are complex and little researched. I urge adults who are considering such a move and who come to me for guidance to take their time. The most difficult problems I've encountered with reconstituted families have occurred where the marriages were sudden. The children had little or no time to get to know one another or their new step-parent. Quite understandably, their natural resentment at the major disruption in their lives is even greater when they feel as if this has been suddenly forced upon them. It seems to them that their own needs and feelings have been ignored. Life as they know it has been tossed upside down, and they have had nothing to say about it.

To avoid such problems, I usually recommend taking maybe two years to ease into the new family. Allow the respective children a chance to grow somewhat accustomed to the idea of a new family, and a chance to become acquainted with the new children they will be living with. Take joint vacations. Visit each other. Involve the children in future plans. If two children from one family will be sharing a room, let them decide, if possible, which room and what it's going to look like.

Give them and everyone a chance to feel their way into this whole new universe.

12

Special Problems

There are a handful of particularly distressing problems that surface in the adolescent years, with varying frequencies, at times quite dramatically: depression, suicide, and two eating disorders, anorexia and bulimia. I will review them in this chapter so that you, as a parent, have a sense of what they entail and how to recognize them from their early warnings signs.

DEPRESSION

Judging from current research, depression appears to be increasing among older adolescents and young adults, certainly in the age group of eighteen to twenty-two, and on up to about thirty. While depression affects almost twice the number of adult women as men, among adolescents it seems to be spread equally between the sexes.

Dysthymia, or neurotic depression, is the milder form of disturbance. It is characterized by a depressed or irritable mood that lingers through most of the day, more days than not over a period of a year.

The official symptoms, according to *The Diagnostic and Statistical Manual of Mental Disorders* (the handbook of the American Psychiatric Association), are the following: poor appetite or overeating, insomnia or hypersomnia (oversleeping), low energy or fatigue, low self-esteem, poor concentration or difficultly making decisions, feelings of hopelessness.

I find these adolescents to be unhappy, functioning at a low level, often somewhat paranoid, feeling that they are not being treated right and the world is not a very nice place to live in. They raise unformed but disturbing ideas, wondering what life is really worth anyway, and show suggestions of suicidal acting out, but not significantly so.

They tend to lose interest rather quickly in new activities, and their problems in concentrating usually lead to difficulties with schoolwork. There can be a self-fulfilling downward cycle in these lives. Without intervention, trouble in school can lead to their flunking subjects and dropping out of school, which leads only to further unhappiness.

In a kind of flailing over their own feelings of helplessness, they may act wildly, desperately, antisocially. They may experiment with drugs, or petty vandalism, or sexual promiscuity, all of which may be their way of crying out for help.

What is called "major depression" is a considerably intensified version of dysthymia. All the same symptoms and behavior may be found but to far greater degrees. There is a serious impairment to functioning. They may not, for example, want to get out of bed in the morning. These adolescents seem to have severe depression triggered by a symbolic loss, such as failing an exam or losing a boyfriend or girlfriend. They begin to withdraw socially, pulling away from friends and their normal social activities. And, ominously, they sometimes start to give away treasured possessions, as if preparing to die.

They show associated biological symptoms. Frequently they suffer insomnia and a loss of appetite, especially early in the day. After a sleepless night, they don't want any breakfast, when they once slept well and ate well. They also develop somatic symptoms, pains and aches and fatigue that resemble the symptoms of chronic fatigue syndrome.

Normally, if you see that your child has a significant drop in grades, is not eating well and not sleeping well, and is making statements like "Sometimes I want to kill myself," you have a group of serious warnings. In my view, they should be assessed by a professional.

Also, be on the alert if you have gone through a divorce that has been bitter, with a damaging shuttling of your adolescent between you and your former spouse, or where your adolescent has had considerable difficulty adjusting to a new parent. In my experience, those ruptures often leave the adolescent in a state of significant depression.

SUICIDE

For the parent of an adolescent, this is the most terrifying of disturbed actions, made more ominous in part by the distorted picture conveyed by tabloids and exploitive television. A teenage suicide, or even better a pair of linked teenage suicides with a pact, makes big news. It also sends a chill down the spine of any parent.

The fact is that suicide takes the lives of relatively few adolescents in the United States, between 5,000 and 6,000 in 1992. But having said that, let me quickly add that any suicidal threat must be taken very seriously. Any talk like "I wish I was dead . . . I wish I could kill myself" is an alarm. Any attempt at suicide, however bungled, is even more so.

Studies clearly demonstrate that those who threaten suicide

are seriously ill, and that even if they are not at first successful, they usually will make another attempt later in life. One recent study showed that of children who were treated after a failed attempt, about 30 percent repeated the effort. Of those who dropped out of treatment, the rate went up to 60 percent. Fortunately, these studies indicate a very low rate of success, only about 2 percent.

Government statistics show a slowly rising curve of successful suicides from the age of fourteen to sixteen, then a rapidly rising curve up to age twenty-five. It then levels off and drops down rather sharply by age thirty to a low level, where it stays until ages fifty to fifty-five, when it rises again.

In the age group from sixteen to twenty-five, suicides rank third as the cause of death. Accidents, including of course those notorious teenage automobile accidents, are first, with some 15,000 deaths. Homicide is second, with about 10,000 deaths.

The pattern of suicide attempts among female adolescents is different from that among males. Females tend to use an overdose of pills or a scratching of their wrists, but not deeply, as a way of calling attention to a conflict and drawing outside help to it.

Quite typically, the adolescent has a problem she can't resolve, a problem that seems so overwhelming—a pregnancy, a failed course, a lost lover—yet she can't seem to ask for help. So instead, she takes a dozen aspirin, maybe even pops them right in front of her mother, the most dramatic way she can think of to solicit outside intervention.

Male adolescents, however, tend to see suicide as the resolution to the overwhelming problem, not a way of expressing it. They resort to more violent means than women. As a result, when they attempt suicide, they are much more likely to succeed. Out of one hundred females who try, only two will succeed. Whereas out of one hundred males, fifty will actually kill themselves.

The highest male adolescent rates are found in the Southwest, and while no one is sure why, it is suspected that the availability and acceptability and commonness of guns in that culture is a factor. Suicide also appears to be more common among middle- and upper-middle-class adolescents, who show a tendency to lose self-esteem and turn their aggression on themselves.

Unfortunately, no one has yet figured out why an adolescent would respond so violently to a problem. What is known is not very surprising: Much of it is impulsive, occurring when drugs or alcohol have been used and defenses are down. Adolescents who attempt suicide are generally rather chronically unhappy and possess low self-esteem. There are also patterns of drug abuse in the families and in the adolescents themselves. A high percentage of suicides occur in families that are chronically dysfunctional and/or broken; bad divorce, foster care, child abuse, and alcoholism are all prominently reflected in the research.

There is no researched correlation between depression and suicide among adolescents, though there is broad acceptance that chronic mild depression is a contributing factor. The act itself seems to be related more to impulsive issues grounded in a bleak view of life and the world.

A recent anonymous letter to the *New York Times* cast light on the darkness of adolescent suicide. It was written in April 1994, when the media were twitching wildly, this time over the suicide of Kurt Cobain, the lead singer of the nihilistic group Nirvana, which was hugely popular with teenagers. It's a letter worth reading.

To the Editor:

Re "Reflections of Cobain's Short Life"
(critic's notebook, April 11): In the press, rock stars who die are remembered primarily as martyrs. Yet, though rock stars may have the public eye and the often unwarranted job of speaking for society, they are only examples of what many of the rest of us feel and live and die with.

Kurt Cobain was another unfortunate young man faced with a lot of responsibility at a young age. He had a family, a business to run, and he was confused, addicted to drugs and responded as many 20-somethings do—with despair and suicide.

I attempted suicide at 26. I landed in a coma for four days from a mixture of heroin, alcohol, and sleeping pills, but I was lucky. I pulled through and got the help I needed. Kurt Cobain obviously didn't.

If you stick around you may find we grow more comfortable in our skin, and the angst of youth slowly fades. Not to say there is not pain later; most of us can attest that life brings both love and pain. And suicidal tendencies are not so much cured as healed and understood.

I imagine almost everyone, suicidal or not, can relate to the overwhelming confusion that comes with the clash of childhood dreams, no matter how grand or small, and the reality of adult life. This hits hard in our 20s. So here we are, adults alive in our dreams, and life still hurts— what's wrong with us? Why can't we feel good about ourselves and our lives?

This is not a virus exclusive to rock stars. Let's not martyrize and glorify Kurt Cobain, as we did River Phoenix, James Dean, or Jimi Hendrix.

Because of my suicide attempt, a lot of people have asked me why Kurt Cobain, who had fame, fortune, love, everything anyone could want, could still be so unhappy. I can understand it, though I did not have any of those things when I overdosed.

All your life you struggle against your unhappiness and bait yourself with dreams of a better life, and as those dreams are attained and become real, you fall into a deeper depression. Love and all things that make people happy are around you, but still out of reach. Before you had those things you could convince yourself circumstances made you sad, but now you've got nothing to blame but yourself. At least I did.

It's so much about self-esteem. The way we are brought up at home and taught in schools. How we treat each other as kids, and how we are treated in turn.

There is a giant aching among today's youth. So much healing needs to take place. Kurt Cobain gave up. I would have too, but I got help.

We all need to take responsibility for ourselves and our sisters and brothers. Suicide is no solution—in this case it means a child will grow up without a father, a wife now has no husband. We all feel pain, not just artists and musicians, but also mechanics, pilots, waitresses, and monks—now, what can we do to start the healing?

—Name Withheld
Brooklyn, April 11, 1994

ISSUES DURING
THE COLLEGE YEARS

The years from eighteen to twenty-five are tough years emotionally. There's a confluence of important issues at this time. First, the search for independence gets pretty well resolved when the adolescent leaves home and goes off to college. Even for the commuter, college marks a distinct mental journey to a new world, provokes a new way of looking at oneself, thinking of oneself.

College brings great new responsibilities. One is away from the protecting if restricting eye of parents and now responsible for oneself and one's behavior. No parent will see the student drink or tell him to be home by midnight. So what he does by and to himself is in his own hands.

Money assumes a new meaning. Awareness of the vast sums his parents may be spending for college creates a new kind of indebtedness and pressure to succeed. Managing a checking account for the first time, confronting the message of a bounced check—a bank is not a loving, understanding parental figure; there are limits that must be observed—and trying to earn money are all new testing experiences.

Intimacy takes on new, sometimes disturbing meanings. Relationships connote more serious, long-term commitments.

Role identity becomes a meaningful concern by the third year of college, a time when the issues of sexual identity are also becoming clarified and settled.

College is frequently a time of threats to the ego, especially for the vulnerable adolescent. Academic demands and competition are often much greater than anything the adolescent experienced before. Flunking the first course in a lifetime can be a shattering blow. Being dumped, having a first major love affair break apart, can trigger mourning and a variety of depressive reactions.

Homesickness surfaces sometimes in unexpected degrees, indicating that the adolescent has still not made an adequate separation from his parents, adding sadness and confusion and anxiety to his state. As college proceeds, there is the role problem of deciding at last what he really wants to be. If he's a C-student in government, not interested in being a lawyer or going to medical school, and his father wants him to go into business, but he despises his father and isn't sure about the business world either, uncertainty becomes ominous.

These are among the implicit threats that surround the adolescent during the college years, and they can certainly trigger emotional problems.

Bulimia, which is binge eating and forced vomiting, seems to flower among women in the first year of college.

The adolescent who is prone to suicide often reveals that tendency in college. All the ego blows I mentioned above can contribute to the student's suicidal condition, and his psychodynamics will determine which of these will have a greater effect on him. A student whose parents are very bright and successful professionals and who fails two courses may find that a more wrenching disaster than losing a girlfriend. This is not to suggest that every adolescent who fails courses in college begins to contemplate suicide. But for those with a suicidal tendency, such a failure will commonly flush it out.

ANOREXIA

For a serious, often life-threatening disorder, anorexia usually starts in the most innocent of ways.

Quite typically, the adolescent girl—90 percent of reported cases are females—has a friend who makes an offhand remark: "You're getting heavy, kid." Or she catches something on TV about diets. Though she is nowhere near obese, perhaps a bit chubby, she decides her time has come. She announces to her family that she is going on a diet.

She starts on one of her own creation. Only each day, her diet becomes increasingly radical. By around the tenth day, she has lost five or six pounds and is eating practically nothing. Her family and friends all tell her how great she looks, but when she stares at herself in the mirror, she is not satisfied. She thinks she still looks too fat. Anorexics always think they look too fat, even when they are a skeleton of eighty pounds.

The diet enshrouds her life. By the time she loses another five pounds, her mother begins to worry. "Dear, don't you think you've lost enough weight? Aren't you getting tired of that diet?"

"No, no, not yet. I still don't look good. I want to get down one more size."

That night, her mother pulls her father into the matter, and the conflict escalates. The girl begins to create ways to fool her parents. Typically, for example, she starts to become much more involved in preparing dinners for the family. Then, at dinnertime, when she barely touches the food, she claims that she ate and ate while preparing it. She might even drink a great deal of water to look bloated and lend proof to her claim. She might start sneaking laxatives, lots of them.

Finally, with the family at war and the adolescent a good twenty pounds underweight, she gets dragged to her pediatrician. Usually, she then undergoes a series of tests and workups, the pediatrician ruling out one disorder after another and ultimately settling on anorexia. This doctor then recommends counseling, which often is resisted by the parents—"Over a little diet?"—as well as the adolescent—"Not on your life. I'm not crazy. There's nothing wrong with me." Denial blankets the problem.

Depending on the parents' own problems and their response to the crisis, by the time they turn to the pediatrician the weight loss may have reached dangerous levels. As much as 18 percent of anorexics die from their self-inflicted starvation.

I recall one of the first cases I encountered, a fifteen-year-old girl, about five feet, eight inches, who weighed fifty-three pounds. It was horrifying to look at her, as if an Auschwitz survivor had somehow floated into my office. For six months, she had been starving herself on a diet of water and diet soda. When I talked with her, she insisted that she was still too fat and her hips were too wide.

We put her in the hospital on a strict regimen of five small meals a day and a behavior modification plan. In her case, it wasn't necessary to tube-feed her or use intravenous treatment, as it sometimes is, or put her in an intensive care ward. As she began to gain pounds, she was allowed privileges. First, she could get out of bed and take herself to the bathroom. Then, she could move about the room. At the next level, she could go out into the ward and after that have recreational therapy privileges. When she had put back ten pounds, she could go up to the psychiatry floor. Finally, her parents were allowed to visit.

She came from a quite disturbed family, which is not always true with anorexics. Her father had signs of being a paranoid schizophrenic, quite preoccupied with mysterious forces that were against him. An extremely obsessive man, he set rigid schedules for the family. Exactly what time each of them used the bathroom, for exactly how long, exactly what time the main course of dinner was to be on the table, exactly what time it was to be removed. Her mother was a depressed woman who silently suffered her husband's needs and demands, and the girl herself docilely existed in this world, wanting to please her father.

Given the pathology of the family, I recommended that the girl be moved from the hospital when she was sufficiently recovered—a process that took about six weeks—to a residential treatment center rather than back home. Her parents agreed, and that enabled her to recover there over the next year and a half. I'm sure she would have relapsed had she gone back into her disturbed family. (With less severe cases and less troubled families, family therapy can enable the patient to return home. If residential treatment is required these days, customarily it runs for three to six months, after which the patient moves to a halfway house.)

A bright girl, she went from the treatment center to college, still keeping her distance from home. I saw her periodically. The last time I saw her, she looked wonderful and was on her way to a Ph.D.

Why?

Though aspects of this case were extreme, it holds elements commonly found in anorexia.

First, there was the deadly combination of exceedingly controlling parents and an accommodating child, the child who has an overriding need to please. This girl had a tyrannical father and a terrified mother, who conveyed to her daughter the quality of being passive and dependent.

It isn't necessary to have all the strangeness of this particular family to have a home in which the control of the parents is pervasive and stultifying, but with an anorexic you will usually find intense control problems and a family that is generally quite disturbed.

The child who must live with that, however, encounters great difficulties when she reaches adolescence. Then she begins to feel the quintessential need of adolescence, the need to become independent in some fashion as her peers are doing. But that powerful drive is in profound conflict with her need to please.

Eating becomes the unconscious solution. It is still one part of her life over which she has control. And by not eating, she defies and causes distress to her parents. That, in a twisted way, is an expression of rebellion and bizarre independence.

From a psychoanalytic perspective, not eating also serves another unconscious desire, which is to remain a little girl. According to this view, the girl is overwhelmed by the demands of adolescence, including the need to separate from her parents and become her own person, to act independently, to experience sexual growth and involvement. Anorexia stunts physical and sexual development. The girl's breasts diminish in size; her menstruation, which has just started, stops. She arrests her normal growth patterns.

And she succeeds in making herself once again dependent on her parents.

Hilda Bruch, a psychoanalyst who did important research on anorexia, wrote a wonderful short book on the subject, entitled *The Golden Cage,* which I recommend for parents and their adolescent daughters.

BULIMIA

Through bulimia is often linked with anorexia in discussions of adolescent eating disorders, it is rather different.

Bulimia entails episodes of binge eating by the adolescent girl—once again, this is predominately a problem for females—episodes that are then followed by forced vomiting. Huge quantities of food are consumed in this eating frenzy, usually sweet food that can be consumed quickly and without much chewing. Ice cream is perfect, and in the course of a couple of hours, the bulimic might churn through a gallon of it. Then stick her finger down her throat. She might also resort to laxatives and over time put herself on a diet or a regimen of exercise to counter the binging.

Unlike anorexia, bulimia is rarely life threatening. A bulimic can discolor or rot her teeth from the hydrochloric acid released by the vomiting, but her weight does not drop off to any dangerous level. Usually the bulimic appears to be of average weight, perhaps a few pounds overweight or underweight, but there is nothing in her bodily appearance, unlike that of the anorexic, to suggest a disturbance.

The bulimic is often concerned with her weight, thinks her life will be brighter if she could be trimmer, more physically attractive. But her sense of her body image is not as distorted as the anorexic's.

Indeed, the bulimic's normal appearance helps her to hide her problem, and as a result it often goes untreated for some time. There is no firm research, but bulimic patients of mine have spoken of how widespread bulimia was during their college years, of how there were always, or so it seemed, one or two young women on their dorm floor vomiting every night.

I have never had an adolescent referred to me because of bulimia, but rather for some signs of depression, which is officially recognized as commonly associated with the problem. The depression affected their schoolwork, quite typically, and so their parents gave me a call. Or the depression seemed to set in when they broke up with their boyfriends. There was no mention or history of eating problems. And then, perhaps six or seven months into treatment, the patient would say: "Know what I did last night, doctor? I ate two gallons of ice cream and went to my bathroom and threw up."

Bulimics are ashamed of their actions. They don't deny their actions to themselves, as anorexics do, but they speak of the guilt they feel while they are binging. And they speak of their elation when they've vomited.

There is uncertainty over the root causes of bulimia. From my cases and experience, I think bulimia is a form of depression, which is how I treat it.

These are adolescents with image problems and related self-esteem problems. When they suffer a blow that sets them back and triggers a depressed mood, they try to soothe themselves by binging. I see them as unconsciously searching for care, needing to be fed and to be mothered. The choice of ice cream as the perfect binging food even suggests a mother's calming milk. They are searching for an oral pacifier, just as certain kinds of troubled men are doing when they go on an alcoholic binge, drinking themselves comatose on a Saturday night.

Bulimia certainly can be treated, and unlike the anorexic, the bulimic will not fight treatment. What I have found successful is individual psychotherapy combined with group therapy. Once the girl uncovers and recognizes the roots and causes of her depression through psychotherapy, her attitude toward herself is altered and she no longer has a need to seek relief through the binge-vomit cycle. The group work with her peers provides insights and encouragement to control her behavior.

13

Getting Help

The Walkers, as I'll call them, came to me with a very common set of concerns regarding their fifteen-year-old daughter, Beth. Once a strong student and a gregarious girl with a number of friends, over the last six months Beth's grades had slumped to the D-level, and she had withdrawn from her usual social activities. She no longer saw her friends—they used to regularly drop by the Walker's apartment after school—or was interested in drama, one of her earlier passions. In fact, she seemed to have no interest in anything, and so far as the Walkers could determine, she spent much of each day in her room with the door closed, listening to music.

Further, they couldn't get her to talk about what was troubling her, which was a fairly typical adolescent response to this kind of disturbing situation. When they finally suggested that she see someone for help, she replied angrily, "I'm not crazy. I don't need any help."

Beth was ensnared in a conflict. She knew she was having problems and feeling down about herself. But she was struggling for independence. To have gone to her parents to talk, to have sought guidance and comfort would have been something of a betrayal of her struggle. It would have seemed to her like an admission that she was not strong enough to be independent. It would have been a narcissistic defeat. Moreover, accommodating her parents, acceding to their suggestion of going for help, would have meant giving in to the very authority figures she was trying to separate from. Instead, she impulsively shouted at them, "I can take care of myself!"

Desperate for guidance, they called their pediatrician, who referred them to me. After hearing their description of Beth's state, when they came to my office, I could tell them that her pattern was common and certainly treatable. But I also had to caution them that adolescents often resist treatment.

I explained to the Walkers that in a situation like this they were perceived by Beth as the adult authoritarian figures against whom her inner struggle for independence was being waged. It would help everyone, I thought, if they could view the problem from her perspective. Also, I told them that in the normal process of adolescent upheaval through which Beth was passing, her own thoughts could begin to seem somewhat questionable, even crazy to her. For example, like other adolescents, Beth was probably experiencing for the first time an active fantasy life, often laden with sexual desires she never before confronted.

In general, it was reasonable to expect that she was at a point where, exploding with new feelings, she was unsure of who she was or what she was becoming. All of this could be extremely unsettling to her and cause her at times to question just how solid she was mentally.

Given her point of view, if they suggested that she needed help, Beth could well have taken the remark as an accusation, a confirmation that she was in fact crazy. Obviously, that could be quite terrifying. For Beth, it could even carry a special threat: her independence would be curtailed. Crazy people, she knows, are subject to controls.

OVERCOMING THE RESISTANCE
TO TREATMENT

I suggested that the Walkers return to Beth and recast the issue. Instead of seeming to place the onus on her, they might suggest that they all have a problem, which they do. The family has a problem. And be specific about it. She is obviously having difficulties at school, and she has withdrawn from her friends and her parents. These conditions, for whatever their reasons, affect us all. We are a family, and one member of the family cannot be going through a rough time without the others being affected.

They should further explain to Beth that because of their concern, they went to see me. And I advised them that, in order to get a grip on the problem, they should all come in and talk with me.

That approach, I told them, was effective much of the time. It removes the stigma from the child. No one is pointing a finger at her, accusing her of being crazy, telling her that she needs a psychiatrist. Now the focus of the problem has shifted. It is a family problem. Now she is one among equals, she and her parents together. It also gives her some sense of control, as well as some respect and status.

If this stratagem doesn't work, I suggested, they can make the school an ally. A call to the school's guidance counselor can quickly forge the connection. The counselor can agree that Beth should have some help or at least get an evaluation. I have had more severe cases where the school counselor together with the school principal went so far as to tell students that they could not continue in school without help.

The help did not necessarily have to come from me, I explained. The school counselor might want them to consult with a professional who works regularly and closely with the school, usually a psychologist, social worker, or lay therapist. These professionals can be fine, though I think a psychiatrist might be best for the initial evaluation of the case. A psychiatrist is, after all, a medical doctor who has a specialization in psychiatry. If there are physiological aspects to a disturbance and/or drugs are appropriate as part of the therapy, a psychiatrist has the training to diagnose and the legal authority to prescribe.

I have also advised parents with troubled adolescents who are away at college to get their children started with the college counselor. And this is one time when I suggest that if necessary they should apply economic pressure: if you don't start getting help, we won't continue to pay your tuition.

Often that is the only pressure available to the parents. If their college-aged adolescent is eighteen or older, the law recognizes him as an adult, even if the parents see him as their troubled, needy child.

Economic pressure doesn't always work. I've had cases where the adolescent had such a strong need to defy his parents, he chose to withdraw from school. That's tough for everyone, but sometimes you've got to wake up in the gutter. Like alcoholics, some of those adolescents needed to shatter themselves before they would take any steps to recover.

In fact, alcohol and drug abuse often are central to these cases; the adolescents become so antisocial and unmanageable they have to be expelled from their own homes. A national parents association called Toughlove can help with these desperate problems. With a network of support groups around the United States, it can be contacted at 800-333-1069.

There is yet another recourse with a truly resistant adolescent, if he is a minor: a court order. Each state has its own name for this—in New York it's a PINS, Person In Need of Supervision. The parent petitions the court, and the court gives an order that the adolescent must receive a formal assessment from a professional, which is to be returned to the court with recommendations that the court can then act upon. It's the same process used in contested divorce proceedings.

I was sure, however, that such a tactic wouldn't be necessary for the Walkers. Try to be specific, I urged them. Point out to her that she had been a very good student, and now something was obviously interfering with her ability to think clearly and work the way she usually did. Wouldn't it make sense for all of them to sit down and try to sort this out?

They might even suggest to her that after sifting through all this, it might turn out that all she needs is some special tutoring to get back on her feet. A suggestion like that is unthreatening. It can help her to look at her problem in a concrete way, allow her to reach a point where she can say, "Well, it's true. I have been having a lot of trouble at school. I really don't know why. But I can't seem to get it together."

Once Beth—or any adolescent—reaches that point, where she can overcome her denial and resistance and admit that there is a problem, she will usually come with her parents to my office. Though, as I cautioned the Walkers, there is no guarantee that she will stay.

ASSESSMENT AND TREATMENT

The process with the Walkers was fairly typical.

In the first session, when I saw them alone, I got a sense of the main problems as well as a rather detailed developmental history of Beth, including a full medical history of her infant and childhood years. She had no childhood diseases like meningitis or diabetes that might be contributing to her existing problems.

I also tried to extract a sense of the family. Was it an intact functioning family? An intact dysfunctional family? They spoke of not being able to get Beth to talk to them about her problems. Did she usually? Under normal conditions, how much communication was there between them and her? What were the usual kinds of problems they had with her?

The picture they sketched was of a reasonably solid family in which there had been an easy openness. They felt they had made themselves available to Beth and she in turn felt comfortable in talking with them, especially with Mrs. Walker, about her life, good and bad.

When they came in with Beth, however, a somewhat different family portrait emerged. That frequently happens in family evaluations. The parents have held one view of their family, quite unaware that their child held another. But the child, in the security of the therapist's office, feeling that she has immunity for whatever she says, unloads for the very first time feelings she has kept hidden.

In Beth's case, she felt that, yes, she probably could talk to her mother, but not to her father. He always seemed to be so judgmental, she felt, and if she had a real problem, she didn't feel comfortable going to a parent who she feared would judge and criticize her, rather than understand and sympathize with her.

In fact, in general, she felt her parents demanded and expected too much of her. She was willing to work hard, she said through tears, but she always felt that no matter how hard she worked she would not achieve what they expected. When she got a B in a subject, she felt they expected an A. When her grades slipped to Ds, she was mortified, too embarrassed to talk about it, even with her mother.

It took a lot for Beth to say that much, to be that honest, and I told her so. I also told her that I was sure she had educated her parents, that they had not been aware of how she really felt, and that without such awareness, they couldn't very well respond to her needs. And they agreed with me.

I suggested to them all that they should talk among themselves about the issues Beth had raised, and that perhaps the most helpful next step would be for me to see Beth alone. By this point, I could see that Beth showed symptoms of depression and clearly suffered from the blow to her self-esteem of this whole experience.

Beth slowly nodded. With more reluctant adolescents, I have to convince them at this point that they should have a chance to express their point of view, that I'd already had a session alone with their parents and gotten one perspective.

The following week when Beth returned by herself, it was clear that there was some movement. The three of them had continued to explore the issues she had raised, and her father had allowed that maybe he was too hard on her, even though he never intended to be. This admission didn't make everything perfect, but it was the first time she had ever heard him say anything like that, and clearly she felt a new if mild sense of empowerment. She had forced him to look at himself in a new way and to admit that he was capable of making a mistake. For Beth, who had been powerless over her own eroding life for months, taking action and seeing some results could be a meaningful antidote.

Exactly what triggered this slide for Beth was not apparent in a single session. She was depressed and generally overwhelmed. There were signs of what is known as a sophomore slump. After doing fairly well in her freshman year of high school, which had been a daunting challenge to her, she didn't work as hard in this, her second year, even though the demands were greater.

Socially, she had fallen out with two of her closest friends, for no particular reason except they all seemed to be growing in different directions. Which happens.

She did feel a greater pressure to date. Beth was not unattractive, if a bit gangly, and while she said that she was asked to this party and that, it was clear that she was not comfortable with this part of her life. There was also a feeling that her parents expected her to shine socially.

I got a sense that there was a confluence of disturbing developments in Beth's life, events that had left her feeling defeated. Certainly, as I had suggested to her parents, she suffered from that typical adolescent dilemma of, on the one hand, responding to her drive for independence and along with it her own internal expectations of herself and, on the other, fearing to approach her parents with the problems of defeat. This left her isolated, depressed, and increasingly anxious. Withdrawal and surrender were some of her responses, and they facilitated a chain reaction, leading, for example, to worse work in school and lower grades, which led to more withdrawal and surrender.

I told her that I thought she could benefit from a series of weekly sessions with me and that if she agreed, I'd propose that to her parents. Again, she nodded slowly.

Her parents enthusiastically supported the idea, when I had them come in without Beth for a session, but they felt the whole family also needed some sessions together. That, I told them, was the way I often worked, and we set up a schedule of one session a week for Beth alone and another one for the whole family together, an arrangement we could review after six months.

Quite importantly, the Walkers and Beth all felt comfortable with the process, with our plan, and with me. They felt they could talk with me easily. That's essential to the success of any therapy. If you are in a similar situation and looking for help, be sure you are comfortable with the therapist. If you don't have that feeling, look around for someone else.

Those four sessions—the first with the parents alone, then one with them and Beth, followed by one with Beth alone, and a final review with them alone—constituted the full assessment.

By that time, we all had a sense of the issues, and we had worked out a form of treatment. I did not recommend a tutor, or any special psychological testing as I do when I suspect that a learning disability might be contributing to problems. Those steps didn't seem appropriate here, though at the conclusion of a typical assessment they might be made part of the whole recommended treatment. When I suggested a review in six months, I made it clear to them not to expect everything to be fixed up by then. I never predict how long treatment will take.

As it turned out with the Walkers, after six months, I continued to see Beth on a weekly basis, but the family sessions were cut to one a month. We followed that pattern for another six months, and then we stopped.

Beth was functioning with a stronger sense of independence, a more comfortable sexual identity, and greater self-confidence. She was more at ease socially, her grades had improved, and her family was a happier place. They might all have problems again that they didn't feel they could handle themselves, and I told them that if they did, to come back for a tune-up. I knew they would. That was important for me, especially with Beth. I felt that she had benefited from her therapy in a way that would leave her receptive to other, perhaps longer-term therapy later in her life. Often with adolescents, that is one of my goals, to leave them with a good feeling about therapy so that if they find themselves seriously troubled in life, they will turn to therapy again and perhaps be ready for a more intensive form of it.

ADAPTING TECHNIQUES

This kind of mix of individual and family therapy worked for the Walkers, and it's a mix I frequently use. So many of the adolescent problems that I see in my office are fed by daily family conflicts. In this case, the Walkers seemed to Beth so judgmental and demanding of her, yet she was unable to express her feelings to them, so they never had a clue.

Ugly divorce fights in which the adolescent is neglected or tossed about in a legal football game require a mix of family and personal therapy, although it can be difficult to get both warring parents in the same room. The results can be better if a shaky family comes in before a divorce erupts. The therapy may not save the marriage, but at least it makes the parents aware of their adolescent's disturbed state, an awareness that can render them more sensitive to his needs when the divorce actually hits.

Or,. to cite another common example, an adolescent struggling for independence confronts rigid parents. Flexibility—willingness to compromise on many issues—is so very important for both parents and adolescent. I've been making this point throughout the book, and perhaps it seems all too obvious by now. But it's not obvious to parents who are rigid by character.

By getting such parents to sit down in the same room with their adolescent and discuss their essential conflict, without casting blame, I can often get parents and adolescent to see for the very first time what is causing them so much grief and so many explosive, destructive battles. And then I usually get them to understand that if each of them makes some modifications, some efforts to bend a bit in the other's direction, perhaps it won't be necessary to live on such a constant battlefield. Perhaps it won't be necessary for a father and son, quite typically, to always be screaming at each other. Perhaps they can actually begin to listen to each other. Perhaps even if the father doesn't approve of a son's plan for a Saturday night, they can find some middle ground—he can go to the heavy metal concert, but he agrees to be home by midnight.

Such changes may not seem like a big deal, but accommodations of this sort can completely alter the dynamics and atmosphere of a family. They will not solve, as psychotherapy can, the deeper intrapsychic problems within each person in the family, but even without that happening, a family can change and its members can begin to live with one another in a relatively civilized way. That can alleviate the state of constant crisis in the home, and with it the pervasive anxiety, and give everyone a chance at peace. With peace, who knows? Maybe new family relationships can be built.

There are different cases where the family may be functioning quite well, and the adolescent's problems are essentially within herself. Sudden failure at school, sexual adjustments, inner turmoil over sexual identity are intrapsychic problems. Then family therapy may not be useful. Personal psychotherapy once or twice a week is more effective.

I am not a psychoanalyst, and though I have been analyzed and any number of my friends and colleagues have as well, I question the use of psychoanalysis rather than psychotherapy for adolescents.

First of all, adolescents have a hard time with free association, the technique at the heart of psychoanalysis in which a patient lies on a couch and says whatever comes to mind without censoring any thoughts or words. That can be an upsetting process for an adolescent, giving up control of himself. Freudians speak of the adolescent's terror of regressing through the process of analysis to some earlier, painful stage of life.

Psychotherapy, on the other hand, is more oriented to the here and now. There is certainly, at least as I practice it, an exploration of a patient's past, especially the patient's relationships with parents, siblings, and other meaningful people over the years. But the focus is more on figuring out and coping with present-tense problems. And the technique facilitates this.

In psychotherapy, the patient is not on the couch but sitting up, usually facing the therapist, and while there may be elements of free association, the process is not structured around it. Rather, it is one that more closely resembles a joint exploration of the patient's problems. The therapist is more directive of the exploration and of possible solutions than he might be in psychoanalysis. And in my view, that is more effective therapy for an adolescent.

An adolescent may also have a problem with psychoanalysis and its abstractions. The ability to think in abstract terms develops all through adolescence. A fifteen-year-old simply may not yet have the skills to comprehend and assimilate the abstractions that are the fabric of psychoanalysis. The very idea of irrational behavior, for example, might elude him.

Also, analysis requires at least three if not four sessions a week. When you add up those hours and tack on the time it takes getting to and from a session, whether it's by crosstown bus or by car, you can see that analysis can devour a large chunk of an adolescent's time. Every child with problems can use help, certainly, but a parent has to balance off the troubled adolescent and the need for therapy with the need to broaden the base of the adolescent's life. This is a time, after all, when peers and socializing and hanging out and clubs and sports and other after-school activities mean so much.

As I noted in the previous chapter, adolescents, being so sensitive to peers, respond very well to group therapy for bulimia and other problems. Peer groups allow them to share their problems and gain acceptance and insights from peers. They can take advice and criticism from them far better than from their parents or other adults, and when peers put pressure on them in groups to change their behavior, say, to stop binging and vomiting, it can be extremely powerful and effective.

With bulimia, then, I try to simultaneously combine group with personal psychotherapy. In personal therapy, we try to get at the depressive roots of a patient's problem, while the group serves to reinforce better eating behavior.

Severe conduct disorders and bad drug problems may require a month or more of residential treatment at the beginning to get them under control.

CONFIDENTIALITY

There is another aspect of therapy, especially therapy with adolescents eighteen and over, that parents should be prepared for. The adolescent may well say to his therapist, "Look, I don't want my parents involved with us. What I have to say is between us and stays in this room."

According to the law, an eighteen-year-old is no longer a child. That means the therapist is legally and ethically bound to provide the adolescent with complete confidentiality. Yet the excluded parents are expected to pay for the treatment.

It is not uncommon for an older adolescent to make such a request. Typically, many of his problems are related to separating from his parents. To him, they are the problem. Nevertheless, for a therapist to honor such a request can be very difficult for parents to accept, and I have had to explain the matter to countless parents. I tell them I simply cannot talk with them about any of the issues I'm thrashing out with their son or daughter. All I can do when they call is to give them generalizations: "His grades do seem to be improving, don't they? And he does seem to be getting along with his classmates better, doesn't he?" None of this is very satisfying, I know, but if results are evident and his life at school is improving, and if he is finally not erupting at his mother every time she suggests anything at all, the parents are at least aware that something positive is resulting from their investment.

Adolescents under eighteen do not enjoy the same legal right, but I feel ethically bound to provide adolescents between the ages of fifteen and eighteen with a level of confidentiality. Unless patients are extremely disturbed, I offer them the right to be in the room when I discuss their case with their parents. Most choose not to join us, but even then I can reassure them because in the vast majority of cases parents are not much interested in the specifics of the therapy. They want broad outlines, a sense of whether treatment is progressing well or not, whether I think their child is getting better or not. They also want to complain, about the way they think I'm handling matters and/or their child, and they usually want more effective guidelines on how to handle their child.

I have had cases in which older adolescents dropped out of college, which puzzled and angered their parents, and then wanted their parents to pay for therapy, even though they were to be totally excluded from the process. I recall one young woman who dropped out of college when a damaging secret affair with a much older professor suddenly collapsed, and so did she. Yet she could not bring herself to talk about her pain with her parents. As much as anything, their desperation enabled them to support her therapy and give her, at my recommendation, a semester to do nothing but find herself. She stayed in treatment for a year and a half, during which time she started college again at a different institution, and later graduated. I'm not sure what might have happened to that woman had she not had her parents' almost saintly forbearance.

14

Extended Adolescence

By the time an individual approaches the age of twenty-five, he should have pretty well resolved the three principal struggles of adolescence: he possesses a sense of independence as an individual, is reasonably clear about sexual identity, and perceives a fairly distinct role to be fulfilled in society.

College has been completed, though graduate studies may be under way. In general, it is a time for taking a large step into the world and toward self-sufficiency. Being able to support oneself financially is a final border of adolescence. It allows one to physically remove oneself from the family's home. It is an affirmation of one's chosen role.

In recent years, largely because of the economy, a growing number of older adolescents, young adults really, have found themselves blocked at this juncture. Ready to take the great next step in their lives, they have been unable to find the jobs they seek. And so they have been thrown back on their parents, back into the home of their birth, forced to remain dependent, to endure an extended adolescence.

For their parents, who were perhaps anticipating a new stage in their own lives—a time when they would be relieved of many of their parental burdens, free perhaps to travel or retire—this is a profound jolt.

For both young adult and parents, it is a highly stressful situation, a turn in life that is full of traps.

Being forced back into the parental home, especially after the freedom of life away at college, is a severe emotional setback for the young adult. His self-esteem and self-respect have already been battered by rejection, by not being able to secure the job he wants. Even that job might have been something of a compromise. By the end of college, he finally gave up a dream: he was not going to discover the cure for cancer, but perhaps he could make a living and find reasonably interesting work at one of the big drug companies. He became reconciled to that adjustment, but then not even the drug companies were available to him—they weren't hiring. Or he might have abandoned the notion that he would reinvent personal computers, but there weren't even low-level openings at existing computer companies.

Defeated, he returned home, battered and depressed.

His parents, though well-meaning, quite typically fell unconsciously into an old pattern: they are the parents, and he is the child. Parents set the rules, children obey them. All of this is terribly infantilizing and contributes to the demoralization of the older adolescent who is, in reality, let us not forget, a young man.

Life under those circumstances is a daily strain for everyone and is potentially explosive. I recall one patient of mine who was forced to live with his parents, both of whom treated him like a child. One day, he drove his father to the airport, and all the way there his father obsessed about the endless daily chores he expected his son to manage in his absence. My patient, who had a history of difficulties with his father, found the idea of the man's reminding him to make his bed and walk the dog three times a day so offensive that he tuned his father out.

This didn't stop the man from continuing his litany, however. And when they were about to part inside the airport, he pulled out a list of all the chores from his pocket, which he wanted to review one more time and leave with his son.

The young man lost control of himself, started screaming and shaking his father. It got so bad the police intervened.

Only after that outburst, and a number of sessions with the whole family, did I get his parents to agree to the solution that works so well in these situations: to subsidize their son so he could live elsewhere.

And this is the direction in which I steer most parents. Whether the young adult is searching for a job or working at one that does not pay very well, it is much healthier for everyone if he can live outside the family home.

Immediately, tension and friction are removed. And the terrible cloud of failure starts to lift. Life may be tough, but at least he does not have to go from living on his own during four liberating years of college to being his parents' little boy. At least his independence is preserved, his self-esteem restored.

Moreover—and this is very important—his sexual life remains private. There is no easy answer to the problem that inevitably arises when the older adolescent moves back home and wants to bring someone home for the night. Most parents find this behavior overwhelmingly difficult to accept, not realizing that it has been a part of their son's or daughter's independence for years. Living apart, this is not an issue.

The separate living space need not be elaborate—a modest studio apartment or three or four friends sharing an apartment. Whatever the arrangement, it clearly supports one idea of successful parenthood: to help your children achieve a successful separation from you. Obviously, money is a consideration here, although there is no question that the separate living arrangement will be far less expensive in emotional turmoil.

RETHINKING LIFE AT HOME

If you cannot afford to set your child up in a separate residence, and she must return home, you can do this in such a way that you respect her needs for separation and privacy.

If you live in a private home, perhaps your basement can be remodeled into a small studio with its own bathroom, kitchenette, and, most important, its own entrance.

Or, with apartments, a room in the back can be remodeled so the young adult has a semblance of privacy and some space of her own, off from the rest of the apartment. This is certainly preferable to being back in her old bedroom right next to her parents.

If the young adult is working, I recommend that she pay some rent, even if it's only a token amount. She can then feel like a contributing adult, and, in my view, her self-esteem will be bolstered.

Whatever the physical arrangements, if everyone is under one roof, compromises will have to be made on both sides, and it is healthy for everyone if this is openly recognized and discussed.

It may be psychologically quite important, for example, for the young adult to lead a relatively independent life with a separate schedule of his own. Family dinners at seven each night may not fit into this plan. Or even when he is home for meals, he may prefer to make them himself. Even parents who can understand the defeat their child is experiencing by having to move back in with them will find it much easier to accept separate schedules and separate lives if everyone sits down and talks about it first.

While it's best to avoid regression to the times when parents dictated all the rules, people who live together do need some rules, and they can certainly be worked out jointly. Perhaps it can be agreed, for example, that Saturday night is a time when the returning son or daughter is free to entertain at home. I have heard of parents who, under such circumstances, make a point of going out on that night or others who are able to go off to their second home for the weekend.

Parents can play a critical role in the older adolescent's recovery. They can understand the psychological blow their child has suffered and, without infantilizing him, show and tell him that they do understand.

They can be honestly encouraging: "Try to look at it this way," they tell him. "They economy stinks, and to be turned down in this economy, this marketplace, is no reflection of your true value of what it would be in a different marketplace. And it certainly is no reflection on your character."

EMOTIONAL AND FINANCIAL SUPPORT

Parents can assure their child that they will be supportive, personally and to some extent financially, until he is able to work through this difficulty. Most important, in this regard, they can encourage him to pursue his basic ambitions and not take the first job that comes along, simply because it is a job.

I have heard of various cases of older adolescents who desperately wanted to work in book publishing. But when the job finally came along, like most starting jobs in publishing, it paid what was practically below minimum wage. This was a moment when parents could make a dream possible.

I recall one case in which the young woman was stunned that she would be making less than her father's secretary. Her parents explained to her that that was the reality of the profession she had chosen. The job was still a way to get started in publishing, and it was a great accomplishment that she was chosen for it. The young woman was living at home and together with her parents figured out what it might cost for her to share an apartment with friends, how much she would have from her meager paycheck to contribute to that, and how much more she would need, which her parents then offered to give her. This was a great opportunity, they said to her, and we've got to help you make it possible.

It is hard to overestimate what a profound ego lift such a supportive response can be.

I once had a patient who wanted to be a screenwriter. The young man had shown talent in college as a writer and during that time made a film with friends that won a prize. But writing movie scripts is not something college graduates, even promising ones, get hired to do in any economy. Usually, they have to write scripts on their own, with the hope of securing an agent who can then try to interest filmmakers in one of the scripts or in hiring him on the basis of one of the scripts. It is a tough field to break into, with lots of competition.

The young man was quite determined, and he had succeeded in attracting an agent but little else. There was not much support at home, either. His father had created a successful clothing business and wanted his son, his only son, to take it over. Their relations became increasingly strained.

Confused, uncertain, somewhat depressed, the young man came into therapy. He discussed the difficulty of living at home at this stage in his life, taking financial support from his father and feeling increasingly obligated to him. He worried that if success as a writer did not come soon, which of course was not predictable, he would reach a point where he would feel so obligated, so guilty, that he would abandon his dream of writing scripts and go to work for his father. At the same time, he knew that other parents helped their sons and daughters achieve difficult and expensive goals. In some ways, I responded, his quest was not so different from asking for help to get through graduate school. He lit up at that idea and left the session thinking about it. The following week he returned with an original solution.

He went to his father and proposed an arrangement. Using graduate school as a comparison, he asked his father to support him for three years. He would move to Los Angeles to be in the middle of the movie business and devote three years to making some kind of breakthrough. That would be his graduate school. At the end of that time, if he had not been successful, he would return to New York and go into his father's business.

His father was impressed. The plan seemed realistic and sensible to him, and a way he could give his son a chance to prove himself and quite cleanly resolve what the man could see was a deteriorating situation between the two of them. He agreed.

In many ways, what was more important than the father's agreement to financial support was his emotional support. To his everlasting credit, he did not simply tell his son he would take a chance on this, suggesting that he was more or less willing to risk a financial investment in his son. No, the man enthusiastically backed the idea, told his son that he thought it was a courageous, terrific thing to try, and continued to encourage him throughout his son's great search.

He was, in other words, a good father, and he and his son were rewarded. This is a story with a happy ending. The young man went west, worked hard, and toward the end of his second year he was hired as a writer for a comedy television series, a show that ran for years, earned him a considerable amount of money, and led to offers for feature-length films.

He remains successful today, and the pattern of his success, made possible by his sound and gutsy proposal to his father and the man's supportive response, is one I like to relate to parents who come to me because of similar conflicts with their own sons and daughters.

SOCIAL AWKWARDNESS

There's another issue of late adolescence that can be troublesome, especially if the young adult is living at home. Many young adults have great difficulty meeting other young adults. The problem is greatest, quite understandably, for people who are shy and for others who have psychological barriers to relating in meaningful ways. Issues of low self-esteem and poor body image can also come into play here. Some people by temperament are slow to make friends.

In college, there is a natural process of socializing. People meet in classes, through extracurricular activities, have a chance to talk and approach one another in relaxed circumstances. A lunch shared or a cup of coffee in a student center allows for contact without much pressure. Dates can be arranged rather easily, and friends are always fixing up friends.

But out in the big, cold world, it is difficult to meet people in such informal, natural ways. There are some opportunities in the workplace, but a singles bar, especially in the age of AIDS, is not a comfortable substitute.

The problem usually becomes magnified if the young adult is thrown back into his parent's home and hasn't yet found a job. Typically, it then becomes their problem. They ask themselves: What is wrong with our son? Our daughter? What can we do to help? They ask their older adolescent, directly or indirectly: What is wrong with you?

Parents call me for guidance, though this is hardly a cause for long-term therapy. But it can be yet another irritant in a stressed family. I try to calm them down. I assure them that their child is not the only twenty-five-year-old in the world to have graduated from college and be without a meaningful companion. Over the many years that I have consulted with students at the medical school, I have lost track of the number of young adults bemoaning the same problem, and they even have the environment of the medical school to ease their way.

I also tell these parents that any efforts they might make to help their children will undoubtedly fail. For if their sons and daughters are reasonably healthy, they will be too invested in their own independence to accept such assistance. Parents can't be matchmakers for their children, not in our culture. By and large, we don't have arranged marriages. A blind date arranged by parents will be strenuously resisted.

Indeed, I caution parents that too much pressure on their children to establish permanent relationships might push them to become overinvolved before they are ready. No one knows how many people get married simply because their parents and their culture expect it of them.

The best thing parents can do is to be supportive and reassuring. This is a painful problem, one that is not easily solved. Assuming it is not rooted in a psychological problem, psychotherapy is not going to help.

The young adult can try the obvious. Courses are offered at universities and museums, and many people take them as much to meet others and socialize as to learn. Political clubs and campaigns and volunteer organizations offer a chance to give something back to society and to meet people who feel the same way. Charities can be interesting and also provide social opportunities.

Over time, this is a problem that tends to work itself out. However, during that rough period of enforced dependence, it can loom quite large for both the battered young adult who returns home feeling defeated and his bewildered, anxious parents.

15

Timeline: A Summary, Year by Year

In this final chapter of the book, I'd like to place the key issues and developments that we've been considering into a time frame. This should give you a slightly different perspective on the material, allowing you to see when particular problems and developments are most likely to occur. In some cases I have summarized; in others, distilled and edited—plagiarizing myself, if you will, in order to review and reinforce my original ideas.

There are also a certain number of subjects that did not fit into our earlier discussion, but which do deserve some attention, and they are appropriately included here.

I hope this chapter will provide an overview and summary, better enabling you to anticipate adolescence.

AGES SEVEN TO TEN

Latency: one last chance

These are years when parents have a last chance to lay the groundwork for adolescence. It is a time when parents can listen to their children, their problems and requests, with a new attention and respect, which should create the foundation upon which negotiations can be developed. Negotiations are the oxygen of adolescence. (During adolescence, it will be critical for your children to feel that you will listen to them carefully, that they can trust you to think about what they have to say, and that you can have a true disagreement with them without becoming angry with them.)

If parents haven't done so already, they can set limits on behavior during latency, a time when children are so anxious to please their parents.

A sense of trust between parents and child should have been growing over the years. It can be expanded during latency, to be drawn upon in adolescence.

The first negotiations of independence

Why can't she be allowed to stay up later? Or take herself to school? She is reaching for increased responsibilities. Your respectful responses will allow her to feel that you are listening to her and that she can negotiate with you, terribly important feelings for her to carry into adolescence. These first negotiations also create terms and conditions that will be further negotiable later in adolescence, an important part of establishing your authority and structure in your relationship and in her life.

Modeling

In latency, children have a great desire to please their parents, and they are becoming finely tuned to the habits and styles of their parents. Increasingly, in conscious and unconscious ways, even while they are tentatively feeling out a new, separate identity of their own, they are identifying with their parents and trying to model themselves on them. This can result in desirable attitudes or not, depending on the parents.

If the parents spend hours and hours watching television, the children will assume that this is acceptable behavior. If the parents smoke, drink heavily, overeat, use drugs, the children will shape their own attitudes around that behavior.

Same-sex attachments

Girls relate to girls during these years, boys to boys, with a certain amount of sexual play and exploration as part of these attachments.

Girls hold hands, hug, kiss, enjoy pajama parties, unconsciously comparing breasts and newly developing physical qualities. Boys horse around in locker rooms and explore their sexuality with each other, playing with each other's penises and occasionally mutually masturbating.

A period of modesty

While there are early stirrings of sexuality, latency in general is a time of modesty. Their cultural heroes are not blatantly sexual. Nakedness is embarrassing, in oneself and one's parents, and latency-age children make their first requests for privacy. They want to undress alone, take a bath without supervision. At the same time, they are proud of their development, the signs that they are approaching adolescence. So they want their first bra, even if there is hardly enough breast development to require one.

Early questions about sexuality

The first signs of development naturally lead to questions. What does this hair starting to grow down there mean? What is menstruation, and when will it happen to me? What does it mean when I have a wet dream?

Many parents are uncomfortable talking with their children

about sexual matters. By the fourth grade, your child's school should be teaching the basic facts of bodies and sex. And there are several books that can be helpful to both parents and children: *What's Happening to My Body?* (one book for boys, one for girls) by Linda Madaras, *Growing Up* by Joanna Cole, *Love and Sex and Growing Up* and *Love and Sex in Plain Language* by Eric W. Johnson. Read small sections, and then talk about them with your child. Expect the first questions about AIDS.

Higher levels of learning, higher expectations among parents

As your child progresses through elementary school, the work becomes more demanding, and your sense of him as student grows clearer. As it does, be alert to the unconscious projection of your personal ambitions and fantasies onto your child. This can warp your choice of school for your child, reflecting your unconscious needs rather than the educational needs of your child.

Watch out for unconscious rejections

At this time when schools are frequently reexamined and changed, I have seen any number of cases in which parents send their child off to boarding school, even when such a move is damaging for the child. It is basically a way for the parents to reject their child and to use the schools to hide their own failures as parents. I do not mean to condemn boarding schools at all, but parents choosing them should examine their reasons carefully. Is it a family tradition, one that the child expects will be passed on to him? Fine. Is it the best educational alternative, given the choice of local schools? Fine.

When special talents flourish

A flair for acting, a passion for the piano, a skill for ballet or ice skating—such talents begin to surface during latency, and while pleasing to see and helpful in developing self-esteem, they raise questions. How much do you want to not only encourage but push such talents? If they are pursued to the exclusion of other activities and options, what is the price your child pays? Is it worth it? Whose dreams are you chasing, your child's or your own?

When a parent is confronted with such a talent and such questions, I believe it is best to proceed slowly. Allow the talent a chance to develop, but in an unpressured manner and not at the expense of other interests. That will give your child a chance to explore just how good she really is, without altering her normal course of activities, and without cutting off the many other options for her life.

A sense of being good

A child should come out of latency with a positive sense of self, with a sense that he is good at something.

It might come from athletics, or scholastic achievements, or being the lead in the school play. But the feeling of accomplishment that will enable a child to feel good about himself as a person should come from somewhere. Otherwise, the child can enter adolescence with serious self-esteem problems.

A parent can nurture self-esteem through positive reinforcement, by remembering how important it is for children to hear compliments as well as criticism from their parents. It is a good rule, especially in latency, to balance anything negative you say to your child with something positive. Don't fake it, because your child will detect the phony. But at some point not long after the critical remark, balance the ledger.

Be alert to learning difficulties. Unless caught and addressed, they can plague a child throughout his educational career and be a source of low self-esteem. Special attention to a problem subject, perhaps a tutor, certainly extra encouragement can help with school and restore self-esteem.

Examine your own goals for your child. If they are unrealistically high, they can contribute to his own sense of failure. That in turn can lead him to seek others who share an unconscious lack of self-esteem.

AGES TEN TO FOURTEEN

Puberty

The physical and biological changes brought by puberty are vast. The child adds inches, pounds, and, most significantly, experiences dramatic sexual development.

While changes vary with each individual, girls normally begin puberty around nine and proceed faster than boys, about two years faster. Boys generally begin their pubertal development around eleven, though some start later. The timing of change in puberty varies for each individual.

For both girls and boys, this is a huge amount of growth in a few years, all of which the adolescent is trying to process, integrate, understand, accept, learn to live with, much of which is quite confusing, threatening, and upsetting. And all of which a parent should be aware of.

To further complicate the adolescent's life, psychological adolescence does not correlate with physical adolescence. A young man may have the body of a professional wrestler, but his mind is still that of a twelve-year-old. A thirteen-year-old girl may have the physical development of a twenty-five-year-old woman, but her psychological development is still that of a young adolescent.

For the first time in their lives, these girls and boys are capable of adult sexual activities. And they have the normal curiosity and hormonal urges to try them out.

Sex and sexuality

Sex is ubiquitous in our society. It is available to your child in the magazines at the corner newsstand and in R-rated movies. Standard TV might limit nudity, but the actions and language of characters are pervasively sexual. Radio call-in shows feature people discussing their sexual problems with astonishing vividness.

Studies indicate that the average age for the first sexual intercourse for girls is 16.2 years of age, for boys 15.7. A recent survey showed that one million teenage girls become pregnant in the United States every year; one out of every ten girls under the age of 20.

Obviously, in this environment, there is a genuine need for children to become sophisticated about sexuality at an earlier age. Certainly, quite open discussions about body parts and how babies are conceived should begin somewhere between the ages of nine and ten. By the time children are twelve or thirteen, they should not only understand the mechanics of the sexual act but begin to comprehend the ideas of intimacy and love that are a part of it. And by this age, they should be aware that there are people of the same sex who have intimate relationships. Today they should also understand the risks involved in unprotected sex, most especially that of AIDS. And though AIDS has overshadowed venereal diseases, they should know that sexual promiscuity can lead to many serious venereal diseases.

Parents are often quite uncomfortable teaching their children about sex, and it will show. The parent, then the child, will grow embarrassed, and the child will be left feeling anxious, wondering what is so repellent and forbidden about this subject.

Parents can explore their own feelings around this issue, but they should also recognize that they do not have to be sex experts in order to be good parents.

Many schools, public and private, have sex education courses as part of their regular curriculum. Planned Parenthood offers books and pamphlets and discussion programs which I have found to be solid and trustworthy. You will want to review such resources yourself, of course, and be sure you feel comfortable with what is being taught. Assuming that you are, you might do what countless parents do and use what the school, for example, is teaching as a point of departure for discussions with your own child.

Books can help get around the awkwardness about sex. Those suggested for latency-age children are also appropriate for early adolescents (see page 186). Also helpful at this age are *You're in Charge: Teenage Girl's Guide to Sex and Her Body* by Niels Lawrenson and two books that answer questions about homosexuality, *When Somebody You Know Is Gay* by Susan and David Cohen, and *Understanding Sexual Identity: A Book for Gay and Lesbian Teens and Their Friends* by Janice Reich.

If you want to use books as tools, don't simply pass them to your child. It will be better to read sections together and then talk about the material.

Try not to avoid the issue altogether. It is central to your child's development at this time. If you do not even acknowledge it, you are pushing your child away and sending a confusing message. Remember, by adolescence your child realizes that his parents are sexual creatures too. What will he think if they seem to deny their sexuality to him? In fact, one of the ways you can make contact on this loaded issue is to talk about your own experiences as an adolescent, your own difficulties coming to grips with what was then your new sexuality.

Their own cultural heroes

Among the early signs of independence, you will find your children selecting cultural heroes that are quite different from yours. They are, in other words, beginning to think for themselves, although not too much for themselves. Their choices are usually shared by their peers. But in their choice of music, movie, TV, and sports idols, they are definitely separating themselves from your own tastes.

For the most part, these figures are rather androgynous, suggesting qualities that are both male and female. The overtly sexual rock stars come later.

Although some differences are being declared, there are often areas that can be shared by parents. A willingness by parents to listen to their children's kind of music reflects an openness that will matter to the youngsters.

Role models reconsidered

Once it was all policemen, firefighters, nurses, doctors, movie stars, and ballplayers. That's what five- and six-year-olds want to be.

Now some reality enters the picture. They look around, becoming especially interested in what their parents do. It's a good time to take your children to your office, let them see what you do when you work. Or take them to an industrial museum.

They are broadening their interests.

Ideas and interests of their own

Children are beginning to take their own ideas more seriously, and they very much want their parents to as well.

Whether explaining why a science course is so terrible, or the reason no one likes poor Mary, your child has thought through her views more fully than before. When she presents them to her parents, she really wants them to listen to her and respect her.

While a responsive parent always listens with respect to her child, no matter what the child's age, listening to a younger child is usually to determine need. Now, listening with respect helps to create self-esteem and establish a connection that will be critical for the adolescent years.

Special hobbies and interests develop. A passion for Egyptian mummies, perhaps, or for every statistic ever squeezed out of the sport of baseball. These are yet another way for the child to express his sprouting independence. "This is my special interest, not yours." Here again, respect and encouragement are sought.

Conflicts and negotiations

Though one hopes that negotiation has started before this stage, its importance now becomes obvious. Parents would do well to incorporate three particularly useful elements in their negotiations with their adolescent: agreeing to disagree, listening with respect, and graded negotiation with graded responsibility.

Learning that you can agree to disagree means that you and your adolescent can have different views on people and the world, and that's okay. You can still respect and love each other.

Not so long ago, no disagreement was allowed. You decided what she wore, watched on TV, the music she listened to—everything.

Those days are gone, and with them your absolute power. Now she will increasingly differ from you and your desires, and resist you as she creates her own identity.

While many parents, quite naturally, resist such a development, if a child is to pass through adolescence and become an adult, she must begin to think for herself and form independent opinions for herself.

Also, there will be issues over which there will be no absolute winner, issues that are best resolved by negotiation.

In addition to teaching the principle of agreeing to disagree, you are in a subtle way teaching tolerance. As she grows older, she will have the idea in mind that people who are different from her, in color or religion, for example, or in the way they dress, can still be terrific people.

Without absorbing that principle, she can be developmentally stunted and an exceedingly difficult human being. As the issues of disagreement become more serious and emotionally loaded, not any longer, say, differences over the choice of books, but now over friends, or sexual behavior, she will not respond in the spirit of negotiation. Instead, she will likely be a fierce and stubborn warrior, engaging you in the most damaging of battles, in which no one ever wins.

Implicit in the idea of negotiation is that you listen to your child with respect. Indeed, not listening with respect is a form of ridicule, and it snowballs. Your child will finally decide that what he says to his parents doesn't matter; they aren't listening. Then instead of negotiation there will be warring sides, and as soon as one side gets three words out, the other is yelling and screaming in opposition.

Actually, when you think about it, if you really value your child, there's nothing more important than listening to him.

Regarding the final element of negotiation—graded negotiation with graded responsibility—you exchange power for a new responsibility from your child. Yes, you say, you may go to that party, but you have to be home by midnight, no matter how late the party goes on.

In my view, there are some issues that ought to be nonnegotiable. For example, anything that is dangerous to self and others. There is nothing to negotiate about drugs, abuse of alcohol, casual sex, and drunk driving.

In all other situations, if a pattern of graded negotiation and responsibility has been established over the years, if the parent has consistently listened with respect to the child over the years, and if both parent and adolescent have agreed that they can disagree yet remain respectful and loving, then the essential elements exist for them to negotiate and work through the toughest of adolescent problems.

Avoid overprogramming

Play is the work of childhood, Erik Erikson reminds us, valuable advice for parents with a need to overprogram their children, pushing them to be overachievers. Time is needed in these years for leisure, for playing alone and with friends, for allowing the imagination to expand and life to become fuller and more interesting. Without it, social and emotional growth are stunted.

Surely, if a child shows real talent and interest in, say, the flute, then it should be encouraged. But one lesson a week is enough. And the rest of the week need not be jammed with lessons in gymnastics, dance, acting, and tennis, not to mention karate.

Absentee parents

With both parents working as the norm, and the number of single and divorced parents increasing, the incidence of children at this age being left to their own devices appears to be on the rise. Unfortunately, they are not yet ready for total independence.

Obviously, economics affects planning here. Whenever possible, the child will benefit from having some adult supervision. If a housekeeper is too expensive, perhaps a neighbor can look in, or the child can attend a day-care or after-school program.

Certainly, if a single parent's work requires travel and stretches of time away from home, some arrangements should be made for those absences. In another era, grandparents were happily available for that duty; perhaps they or some other relative can help out now. If not, a special sleep-in arrangement with a person the child likes might be worked out, and best if it is the same person who fills in for the parent for each absence.

Unanswerable questions

By the end of this period, children become aware that their parents do not know everything, and that there isn't a concrete answer to every question. This is especially true for their questions with religious roots: What does God look like exactly? Where does the Trinity come from? How could the Red Sea really be parted?

It would be nice if parents would reply honestly and easily, that they "don't know." But frequently, what comes out if parents don't know the answer is a defensive retort, like, "I really don't have time for that."

Often what is bothering them when this happens is that their authoritarian omniscience is being challenged, perhaps for the first time. But this is the inevitable beginning, the inevitable cracking of that Olympian position.

Defensiveness is understandable, but what would be much better for everyone is a response like, "I'm not sure. Why don't we look that up together?"

Social graces

At this age, children can grasp the logic of good manners, how to behave in a restaurant, how to talk to people, how to treat people, what clothes are appropriate for which occasions. Their interest in the larger social world of adults is expanding. And they can understand that there are certain expected forms of behavior in that world.

To be sure, this is an area that can be overdone. Children can be intimidated and battered until they perform the rituals of "being good in public." But such punishment only warps the child and is not necessary.

Instead, the lessons of social behavior, which are part of growing up, can be conveyed calmly and through parental modeling.

Money

This is a good time to start giving allowances. Children are now able to learn how to manage their money, develop a sense of responsibility for it. Small bonuses for special jobs send the message "If you do a job, you get paid," which is a connection with the work ethic of the grown-up world. Savings can be encouraged.

Obviously, at this age the amount you give is not going to be very much, enough to cover basic expenses of getting back and forth from home to school, perhaps after-school snack money, and a bit of discretionary spending money. It will be useful to talk with other parents and get a sense of how much allowance your child's friends are getting. You set your own amounts, but having an idea of common practices can be helpful, and you can be sure that your child will be very familiar with what each and every friend is receiving.

Working out the amount with your child shows her a new kind of respect and allows her to see how a real budget is figured out. It gives you both a nice chance to discuss what is needed and what is frills, and to negotiate a bit.

It can also convey to her your own concern for money. Parents often complain that their children are growing up these days in such a consumer society, they are so assaulted with ads and enticements to buy, buy, buy, that their children lose sight of the value of money. "We're not poor," goes a common complaint, "but I'd like my daughter to understand that we're not millionaires either, and there are limits."

She will learn a lot by the way you handle money yourself. Extravagance breeds extravagance by example. An attitude toward spending can be expressed in a comment like, "I feel really good about this dress. Not only do I love it, but I got it at a really good price. I shopped around." Every purchase does not have to be justified to your adolescent, but keep in mind the example you are setting. When one couple I know bought a second home in the country, they made a point of telling their son that they had been saving for some years for this and waiting until the real estate market became favorable to buyers, as it had. This was a place they all would enjoy, they told him, and a very good investment.

Many parents have a hard time saying no to their children. That can involve deep feelings, perhaps guilt over real or imagined neglects they inflicted on their children in earlier years, perhaps responses to neglect they suffered many years before with their own parents. You may be able to figure out for yourself why you have this problem, or you may need some help to get at the root causes, which can be many.

One way or another, it is meaningful and helpful to your adolescent that you can set limits, that you can say, "Sorry, I got you two pairs of jeans and a new jacket just last week, and that's it for now." You can add whatever seems appropriate: that you can't afford anything more just now, for example; that enough is enough, even if her best friend is always buying and buying. If you go shopping with her, it is important to say, "Sorry, that dress is simply too expensive. Let's look elsewhere. I'm sure we can find something you like that's more reasonable."

At first, you may well encounter opposition, pouting, and stubbornness. "Oh, forget it, I just won't get anything." But quite soon, I think, such behavior will diminish and then disappear. I think you'll find an acceptance that for her there are limits, regardless of what she may see on TV or among desperately needy friends who do not have limits set on them. And, further, she will realize that she can work with you within those boundaries.

A bit of organization

During this stage, young adolescents are able to start managing their time and lives to some extent. They can be encouraged to realize that there is a time to play, a time to read, a time to do homework. And to plan for tomorrow's quiz, which won't take care of itself.

Checklists by the door can help, and so can rewards. A friend's daughter desperately wanted a pet bird. She was a wonderful ten-year-old, bright and funny, but terribly absentminded and easily distracted. If she didn't forget her books in the morning, she forgot her bus pass or her sweater. Notes to or from school were found days later in the bottom of her book bag, when that itself wasn't misplaced.

A deal was struck: If she could review a checklist each morning and remember her basic stuff as well as her violin and music every Wednesday, and do that for a month, she could get a bird. If she couldn't remember, if she couldn't manage her life to that extent, she couldn't possibly be responsible for a bird. It worked wonderfully, and after the bird arrived, the checklist system was still used effectively, until it wasn't needed any longer.

Family habits

Establish family habits, customs, and special events that are fun for everyone. Dinner together every night is a good example. The meal doesn't have to be fancy, but it becomes a time when the family is together and everyone has a chance to share news and air problems. Maybe Saturday or Sunday afternoon is family time, when the family goes somewhere together. It might be to a movie, or a museum, or a mall.

All of this strengthens the family and the child's connection to it. It can be very effective when children are between the ages of ten and fourteen. After that, in the course of normal development, they begin to lead their own lives more. A weekend afternoon becomes an important time with their friends; a trip to the mall is a social moment, a chance to hang out with girlfriends and boyfriends.

AGES FOURTEEN TO SIXTEEN

Shifts in parental power

During this stage, the nature of parental power is clearly changing. The days of ruling by edict are long gone. Now is the time to appeal to your adolescent's developing, rational mind.

This is not to suggest that parents no longer have controls over their adolescent's behavior and life. There are three especially meaningful controls, which are powerful and easily abused.

The first and least severe is docking, the limiting of privileges. For minor problems, you might want to limit TV time or the use of the phone.

More extreme is grounding, cutting your adolescent off from friends, shutting off the teenager's social life for a period of time. This house arrest is extremely painful to an adolescent. Whatever the cause, try to be realistic when grounding. If the sentence is too long, more than a week or two, you will be nurturing a deep sense of injustice and resentment that will probably fester and grow and ultimately erupt into fights.

The third control, potentially the most damaging, is economic. If you cut your adolescent's allowance, you not only limit her activities but you remind her, at the very time when she is struggling to create an independent self, of how dependent she still remains on your largesse, no matter what she imagines to the contrary.

In applying any of these controls, try to factor into your judgment the reality of the environment of our times. For example, can you censor a child who is over fourteen? Or, more to the point, is this the kind of issue over which you want to try to impose controls and punishments? The challenge for parents is to make their views known without seriously distancing their adolescent and losing a sense of trust in one another.

When it comes to control, there is a danger for parents of not being able to evaluate their own needs and problems and separate them from what makes sense for their adolescent. An adolescent certainly needs continued guidance from his parents, but he must also feel that these are parents with some grasp of what he is going through, what the reality of his world is, and what is acceptable behavior among his peers. Otherwise, their attempt to guide can result in pushing their adolescent away from them.

Affecting this effort is a significant adolescent development that occurs around the age of fourteen: psychologically, he begins to view himself much more as an adult. Physically, he is much more like an adult as well.

Increasingly at this time the adolescent begins to feel he knows what is best for himself, that he is able to do so much more, especially so much that had been denied him before because of age.

So if you say no and your reason is because the activity is for adults only, you run the risk of making the request all too tempting. There is a part of the adolescent at this age that holds back, that still wants to be treated like a child. But there is another new, assertive part that says he should be entitled to the privileges of adults. As a result, you will find you have to make new evaluations. If you ban a particular movie, are you pushing him into sneaking off and seeing it? Compromise becomes increasingly important.

Your new evaluations might not be limited to a concert or an individual movie. More and more you begin to think about what kinds of activities concern you the most, so you can use your influence and remaining power on them. More and more you will think in terms of big priorities and little priorities, not a matter of lists but a reflection on a broad perspective.

So, for example, issues that touch the health and safety of your adolescent might all be considered big priorities. The rest are consigned to lesser importance. Drugs, smoking, drinking, sexual behavior are all clearly then big priorities. But the substance of movies, the media in general are deemphasized.

Not only can such an approach help you and your adolescent to focus on the truly important issues, it can cut down greatly on damaging power struggles that arise over relatively minor matters.

Sex and peer pressure

Peers at this age can pressure an adolescent into sexual activity. For many children, being an accepted member of their own group is tremendously important, even if it means violating the social standards of their parents.

This new attitude frequently becomes a fundamental struggle between you and your child.

Must you lock your daughter up in the tower? Or can you talk to her?

If you have a reservoir of goodwill that has been filled over the years, your relationship with your adolescent should be imbued with a sense of trust. And with that, you can talk with her and be heard.

What you say at the critical ages—fourteen, fifteen, sixteen—is probably going to be most persuasive if it is informative as well as deeply felt.

Self-identity and increased separation

The tensions of what psychoanalytic theorists call the adolescent Oedipal conflict increase. The unconscious sexual pull of a boy toward his mother, and a girl toward her father, grows stronger. As the incest taboo also presses unconsciously, the emotions become increasingly more disturbing, driving adolescents away from the parent of the opposite sex. As a result, the young man will no longer unconsciously feel that he is competing with his father for the affections of his mother, or the young woman competing with her mother for her father. Their focus will turn to their peers. It is there that each will find new objects of sexual, emotional attraction.

Building on his self-confidence, the adolescent begins to recognize that he is good at various activities, courses, sports, perhaps that he is popular. Such feelings and realizations fuel the idea that "now I can be a good person with interests of my own, a person who's different from other people, certainly different from my parents." And with that, the need for appreciation and approval from parents diminishes, and he begins to develop meaningful interests that are not those of his parents.

The effort to break away and be different from parents will be powerful and take many forms. It might be demonstrated in the choice of clothes. And in general, removing oneself from parental rules and controls becomes important.

Parents faced with these changes would do well to be flexible, while still providing guidance. Distinguish between small issues and large ones. Decide what ought to be a confrontation and what needn't be. Certainly any activity that is potentially dangerous to the adolescent or others requires confrontation. For example, the issue of experimenting with drugs or alcohol will call for serious discussion and perhaps discipline. Wearing strange clothes will not. Lose the little skirmishes and win the big battles.

The ability to abstract

Mental development at this age allows for the ability to comprehend abstractions, which leads to a reexamination of many previously held ideas, especially ideas accepted by the parents. Religion, politics, justice, right and wrong are all reevaluated and frequently debated with parents.

While this tendency can present difficulties for parents, the ability to abstract also offers great educational opportunities for stimulating their child's interests, to encourage questioning, and indeed to reach a whole new level of communication with their adolescent.

A stimulating home environment will expose the adolescent to books and music, to museums, to theatrical shows and ballet. She is now receptive to a message that this kind of environment conveys, a sense of human achievement and possibility. Implicit in this message is the idea that she can become anything she wants.

Privacy

Having a private life is part of the struggle for an independent identity, and this extends to the right to have one's own thoughts as well as one's own space.

If the adolescent has her own room, and the door is shut, knocking before entering will show that you respect her privacy. Not messing about in her dresser drawers where she might have her secret letters shows respect for her property and privacy.

A fourteen- or fifteen-year-old might bring certain sex matters to you, ask you about AIDS, or how adults have intercourse, or at what age you think it's okay to have sex. But children of this age will not discuss their own sexual fantasies or confide in their parents as they do with their friends. There are some matters they feel are too personal, and they don't feel comfortable sharing them with their parents.

That need for private boundaries is only natural and ought to be respected by parents. Indeed, recognizing it is one of the early ways of letting go.

Self-centeredness

Around the ages of fifteen and sixteen, adolescents usually are intensely focused on themselves and rather dramatically so. Everything in their lives is very urgent, very important, essentially a matter of life and death.

Parents are frequently irritated by the demanding attitude and the emotion attached to matters that seem to them so minor. Conflicts can easily erupt.

Drugs and alcohol

By this time, let's hope your adolescent understands that drugs and alcohol can be severely damaging.

Nevertheless, expect a small amount of experimenting. She will try a drink or two; she will smoke a joint as well as a few regular cigarettes.

As minor as these experiments might be, it's best to confront your child about them. If you're not sure, you can ask her if she's been somewhere where people were smoking, for she seems to smell of smoke. In this way at least alert her that you're aware.

Unconsciously, your child wants you to be aware; she is sending you a signal for help. Drugs and alcohol are now part of the world around her, and peer pressure aside, she is confused and frightened. She wants your guidance.

Instead many parents fall into a state of denial.

If a party is being given, it's a good idea to check with the parents of the adolescent who is hosting to be sure that there will be an adult on the premises while it's going on. If the party is in your home, don't feel you have to put on a police uniform. Simply being there, greeting people as they come in, perhaps reading or watching TV in your bedroom, occasionally strolling through the place to get a cup of coffee or whatever from the kitchen, will be sufficient.

Set the basic rules for the party beforehand with your adolescent who is host: No drugs or alcohol. You might remind your son or daughter that you as the responsible adult in the home could be held legally responsible if anyone from the party got drunk, say, and had a driving accident afterward.

Many parents tell their adolescents that if they end up at a party where things get uncomfortable because of the amount of drugs and alcohol being used, they should call home and a parent will pick them up, no questions asked. Certainly, if the friend or date who drove them to the party gets loaded or high, the adolescent should call for a ride home and not risk an accident with a drunken or otherwise disabled driver.

If the adolescent gets loaded or high, the procedure would be the same: call to be picked up, no questions asked. But if this happens, or the adolescent comes home drunk, as will probably happen once, the matter should be approached only after everyone has had a chance to recover. The first time this happens, the event can be acknowledged by everyone, but it's best not to hold a Supreme Court hearing. A warning is effective: if this happens again, you will be docked of all social activities, including phone chats with friends, for two weeks. Let your child know that you are very disappointed in him and concerned for all the reasons he already knows.

If, however, this behavior begins to occur with some regularity, the issue is obviously a serious one. Discussion may help. Grounding or some other punishment may be appropriate. But you may also want some professional help to derail this behavior before it becomes too damaging.

Difficult though it will be, you will have to be confrontational and firm with your adolescent. And you may even have to put him in a treatment program, possibly a residential program.

Parent support groups can be very helpful through all the stages of this problem. They can be informative and strengthen your position with your own adolescent: if you and the parents of his friends are united in attitude, the impact will be strong. Together you can also decide which parties, clubs, and the like are acceptable, and which are not.

Socializing in the suburbs

The age of fourteen and fifteen are distinguished by an impressive growth in socializing. It starts with adolescents hanging out with a peer group of the same sex, then develops slowly into hanging out with a mixed peer group. In the suburbs, this whole sexual, cultural development is terribly complicated by the logistics of everyday life, quite simply, how to get around when you're too young to drive.

This becomes a serious problem. I have seen any number of adolescents who feel isolated and depressed because they literally cannot get around. Their friends live too far away, the mall is too far away, there are no buses in their town, and their parents are not available to take them.

I do not think that hanging out in a mall is the most wonderful, mind-broadening experience, but if that's where everybody else is, it's better for an adolescent at this age to be there than moping alone at home.

Some parents have told me that the suburbs are a wonderful place to raise children but a terrible place for adolescents. Responsible parents must get their adolescents around. Some arrange rotating carpools, switching weekly assignments with other parents. Some work out compromise schedules so that Fridays, Saturdays, and one other day, they will be available to transport their adolescents to where the action is.

It's a bother, but it's important for the healthy social development of their sons and daughters.

Mobility and independence in the city

Cities offer the public transportation systems that suburbs often lack, but these days the price for them is safety.

By the age of fourteen, urban adolescents should be given more freedom of mobility. If there is concern over the safety of the subway, the bus can be the way to get around.

Certainly by this age, adolescents can be taking themselves to school alone and be allowed to go to a friend's house after school. Going to the movies with a group of friends should be allowed, and the idea of traveling in groups encouraged. By fifteen, surely by sixteen, the adolescent ought to be allowed to go to a movie, play, or party at night, especially if traveling with friends. You can discuss parts of town to be avoided, although most likely your adolescent will be well aware of them.

In New York, I know, and probably in other cities, taxis are advisable for trips later in the evening.

Granting this freedom enhances adolescents' sense of their own worth and sense of identity: "See, I can take care of myself," they can say to themselves, and really feel it. They are growing up and being trusted.

Going steady

In my view, going steady at this age should be discouraged, which may not be the easiest thing to accomplish. It does, temporarily at least, cut the daunting risk of being alone, or being rejected, both powerful fears. Also, there are some adolescents, and this seems to be especially true with females, who are by temperament unable to play the field, who need deep attachments.

Still, as I have pointed out to many adolescents, going steady limits their options. These are years, after all, when they should have a chance to meet and date all kinds of people. How else can they discover what sort of person they are really most comfortable with? It is a process that begins in high school and continues into college.

Also, steady relationships greatly increase the likelihood of sexual intimacy. Depending on the adolescent, this can be a powerful argument against going steady. But a parent has to be sensitive to her adolescent, usually adolescent daughter, over this matter. If the young woman has, for example, spoken of the sexual adventures of a friend in rather disapproving tones, she might be conveying the message that she herself would just as soon wait before having such an involvement. In that case, pointing out to her that sexual intimacy is one of the likely consequences of steady dating could raise a serious question and a barrier.

Sophomore slump

In the first year of high school, the adolescent typically feels special pressures: a new setting, a more demanding academic program with considerably more homework, the need to make new friends.

Typically, when the challenge is met, the adolescent feels increasingly comfortable in this new environment, confident he will do okay academically, secure among his new peer group.

By the sophomore year, with the pressures removed and social issues becoming ever more predominant, there can be a tendency to focus less on academic work and more on social activities.

All of this comes at a time when adolescents are looking for more independence, responsibility, privileges. Parents may well have to do some balancing between that pull and the sophomore slump. For example, homework still has to be done, and there's no socializing on Monday through Thursday nights; what's allowed on weekends can depend on how the academic work is going.

The work ethic

The principle of earning extra money for doing certain chores should be established by this age. And its importance increases with age. More should be expected of adolescents, and they should be paid accordingly. If they don't want to go to summer camp, for example, they shouldn't loll around the house watching TV. They should try to find some work. They should pay some of the expenses for their clothes as well as their luxuries.

Obesity

Obesity is a curse of our culture. It is so widespread and so rooted in cultural attitudes that it is not considered abnormal, even though it is physically dangerous.

For generations, we embraced the idea that fat equals health, that eating heavily signifies well-being, even success. It is the poor, after all, who do not have enough to eat. It is the thin, ravaged kids who were on the posters of TB campaigns. It was the immigrant parents who never shook the memories of near-starvation days in the old country, who overloaded their family tables and overfed their own children.

A child learns to eat at the family table. Eating habits acquired over years are not going to be changed overnight. Commonly, diet fads promise overnight loss, overnight change, instant gratification, but they don't work. They can't work. By crashing on 1,200 calories a day from a liquid diet, little packs of powder with water added, one can lose weight. But, as Oprah Winfrey has shown us all, that weight comes back as fast as it goes off.

Obesity for an adolescent is a loaded problem because dealing with it can so easily lead to a power struggle. In chapter 12, I discussed eating disorders and noted that anorexia is part of the adolescent's independence struggle. Eating is one part of her life that she can control. If she barely eats at all, she is demonstrating tremendous independence.

If a parent tells a fourteen-year-old, for example, that she ought to lose weight, the remark can damage self-esteem and ignite a power struggle. The battle may be especially bitter since the adolescent can readily see that she is overweight at least partly because of the food that the parent has been serving her for years. Since the girl is deeply involved with her push for independence, anything suggested by a parent can cause an automatic counter-reaction.

It is far better if the advice comes from the adolescent's pediatrician. I believe in conspiring with this doctor, even if it is difficult at first. The pediatrician will probably question you about the kinds of foods you put on your family table and rightfully make you feel awful for serving such rich foods for so many years. The pediatrician will also make you realize that any change for your daughter requires a change in the way the whole family eats. She is not going to lose weight and change her eating habits unless the whole family joins her.

At her next regular checkup, the pediatrician can sit down with her alone and discuss the need to lose weight. The problem is then presented in an appropriate medical context, which is certainly very different from a parental lecture. The pediatrician's medical views and advice will land on receptive ears. A fourteen-year-old who is overweight knows it. What she hears confirms what she knows and gives her strength to do what she knows she ought to do.

When she then comes home and announces that Dr. Sam told her she has to lose weight, you have been welcomed to join her in fighting the problem, and together you can work out ways of changing the diet for the whole family.

One psychoanalytic theory, which has been debated, holds that obesity might also stem from unconscious psychological problems, an unidentified need to gain oral satisfaction. In this case, the nourishment the adolescent is searching for may not be what the food provides her but an emotional nourishment she never received from her parents when she was an infant.

Through psychotherapy, the adolescent can unearth her perceptions of early deprivation, and by understanding it and how it continues to haunt her, realize that her overeating is not going to replace the affection of withholding or unresponsive parents. And then she will be able to change her eating pattern.

Peer support can be very helpful in this process of change. Group therapy, Overeaters Anonymous, and Weight Watchers can all be effective.

AGES SIXTEEN TO EIGHTEEN

Sex

By this age, adolescents should be well acquainted with the fundamentals of sex: they should understand intercourse, pregnancy, birth control, AIDS, and other sexual diseases.

Probably by this time, an adolescent female will have asked for her own gynecologist, one different from her mother's. This request is a meaningful step toward independence. Countless young women have told me they felt inhibited in discussions with their mothers' gynecologists. They didn't trust the doctors to keep matters private. With her own gynecologist, however, a young woman will feel free to ask any remaining questions she may have about sex, and that includes guidance on contraception and birth control.

While the laws vary by state, up to the age of eighteen an adolescent generally needs parental permission if she is to receive a contraceptive device from a physician in private practice. But in many certified public clinics, she can receive a device without it.

By this time, your adolescent should be clear on your views of sexual intimacy, including the age at which you find it acceptable for people to have intercourse. Not that you are going to be able to enforce your views. Increasingly, adolescents are now asserting their own will and control over their own sex lives.

There is typically some initial sexual exploration now, a lot of petting and a certain amount of sexual intercourse. Recent studies indicate that the average age for the first sexual intercourse for girls is 16.2 years of age, for boys, 15.7. There is some evidence that AIDS has caused something of a change in attitude and a drop in the number of adolescents engaging in sexual intercourse.

Parents faced with the sexual independence of their adolescents share a difficult dilemma. They are normally quite anxious, as indeed their sons and daughters are, over this momentous development. But the parents also normally realize that they have to let go, to allow their adolescents to grow up.

Taking this necessary risk is somewhat easier if parents feel their adolescents know the basics about sex. And, of course, if they can also feel that their sons and daughters by this age have some sense of responsibility for themselves and for their actions toward others.

Abortion

Surely, one of the most shattering moments for any parent is when her adolescent daughter comes to her and says she thinks she is pregnant.

If you are faced with this problem, try to remain calm and sensible, as difficult as that might be. Lectures can come later. Your daughter is in urgent need of guidance; she needs to know her options.

If she is telling you about unprotected sex that occurred the night before, one option is the "day-after" pill. Though this fact is not very well known, a contraception pill like Ovral will usually prevent fertilization if it's taken within seventy-two hours of intercourse, for two days at triple the normal dosage. This is not, however, the approved use of the medication, so if you are considering it, discuss the matter with your family doctor, pediatrician, or a gynecologist, all of whom can obtain it for you.

Abortion itself is obviously another option, assuming your adolescent is in the first sixteen to twenty-four weeks of pregnancy, depending on the laws of your state. A gynecologist can explain the operation, and that is a meeting you should offer to attend with your daughter. If she objects, it's probably best that you respect her wishes. At least she will know that you are supporting her at this time when she needs your complete support.

The staff at your local branch of Planned Parenthood can also explain the abortion process and offer clinical services. And they can provide abortion counseling, which includes discussion of birth control and sensible approaches to managing a lifestyle in order to avoid unwanted pregnancies in the future.

Coming out

This is frequently a time when adolescents declare themselves to be homosexual. I have seen more instances of this happening after the adolescent has started college and is living away from home for the first time. If the adolescent has found a special partner and wants to bring this person home, he may decide he has to talk about his sexuality with his parents.

I have never dealt with this situation without the parents being stunned, even though homosexuality seems to be so much more out in the open than it was, say, ten years ago.

When a family comes to my office under such circumstances, I try to explain to the parents that no one really knows the roots of homosexuality, whether its cause is genetic or psychosocial, and that I cannot make their son or daughter "better." I cannot make homosexuality go away and change their adolescent back to a "normal" person. Nor can anyone else.

What I can do, or try to do, is help them all to understand what has happened and to adjust. It doesn't always work. In some cases the parents cannot accept their sons or daughters any longer and actually disown them. In other cases the sons or daughters have a need to angrily bash their parents with their declarations.

Drugs and alcohol

There is less and less adult supervision during these years, which often include the first year of college, the first year of living away from home. It is during this year, flushed with freedom, that so many adolescents endure what is almost a rite of passage: a night in which they become so drunk and sick they want to die. The experience is commonly an educational one.

Persistent alcohol and/or drug abuse, however, is a different matter. With a child over eighteen, your controls are limited. Of course, you try to persuade the young adult to get treatment. But if that doesn't work, what should you do? I have counseled parents to stop sending money, for it was only supporting the drinking and drugs.

Suicide

Though relatively few adolescents commit suicide—between 5,000 and 6,000 in the United States during 1992—any suicidal threat must be taken very seriously. Any talk like "I wish I was dead; I wish I could kill myself" is an alarm. Any attempt at suicide, however bungled, is even more so. Studies show that people who make suicide attempts and do not succeed are likely to try again later in life.

Anorexia

The typical anorexic has an overwhelming need to please her parents, who are exceedingly controlling and domineering. But she encounters great difficulties doing so as she moves along in adolescence. She begins to feel the quintessential need of adolescence, the need to become independent in some fashion as her peers are doing. But that powerful drive is in profound conflict with her need to please.

Eating becomes the unconscious solution. It is still one part of her life over which she has control. By not eating, she defies and causes distress to her parents. That, in a twisted way, is an expression of rebellion and bizarre independence.

From a psychoanalytic perspective, not eating also serves another unconscious desire, which is to remain a little girl. She is overwhelmed by the demands of adolescence, including the need to separate from her parents and become her own person, to act independently, to experience sexual growth and involvement. Anorexia stunts physical and sexual development. Her breasts diminish in size; her menstruation, which has just started, stops. She arrests her normal growth patterns. And she succeeds in making herself once again dependent on her parents.

Anorexia can be life threatening. As much as 18 percent of anorexics die from their self-inflicted starvation. Hospitalization and intravenous feeding may be necessary to stabilize the anorexic, after which personal and family therapy can be effective.

Bulimia

Bulimia entails episodes of binge eating by the adolescent female—like anorexia, this is predominately a problem for females—episodes that are then followed by forced vomiting and/or the use of laxatives. Huge quantities of food are consumed, usually sweet food that can be consumed quickly and without much chewing. Ice cream is perfect.

While there is uncertainty over the root causes, from my experience I think it is a form of depression, often motivated by a feeling of loss of control and low self-esteem. A blow sets them back, triggers a depressed mood, and they try to soothe themselves by binging.

They seem to be unconsciously searching for care, needing to be fed and mothered. The choice of ice cream as the perfect binging food suggests a mother's calming milk, the oral pacifier.

Cars

A parent is probably not the best person to teach an adolescent how to drive. A professional instructor, in a high school course or a private one, has no emotions invested in the experience. He can objectively evaluate the adolescent's skills. For a parent, the experience can be emotionally loaded. The parent may be conflicted over this symbolic step into adulthood that their adolescent is taking, worried about potential accidents before the teenager is even behind the wheel. The anxiety of it all can be divisive.

Once a license is obtained, go along on a number of car trips before allowing your adolescent to use the vehicle alone. Set conditions on driving, and make them clear from the beginning. For example, explain that you will pay for the additional insurance coverage, but your adolescent is responsible for his own expenses: gas, repair bills for any scrapes or other damage he causes, any tickets. He won't drive again until his car debts are paid off.

Accidents and/or speeding tickets require harsh responses. The death rate among adolescent drivers is high. This is a dangerous age, characterized by a feeling of omnipotence: "I can do anything. Nothing bad will happen to me." Much has been written on the car as an extension of the adolescent personality, as a phallic symbol, on speed as a reflection of freedom. The theories are interesting, the statistics disturbing.

I have known a number of parents who have stripped their adolescents of the privilege of the family car after a disturbing ticket or accident: "You haven't shown us that you're responsible. Until you do, I'm not going to spend an extra thousand dollars for insurance. Change your behavior, show us that you're a responsible young adult, and I'll cover you and you can use the car again. Until then, no. It's too risky."

I have also heard of parents who make that tough judgment even before there is trouble. They don't think their son or daughter is mature enough to drive, legal age or not. Too frivolous, careless, happy-go-lucky. They delay the use of the family car. Then as the adolescent gets older and seems to grasp the special responsibility of driving, they allow the use of the car but on a limited basis.

The college choice

Choosing a college is one of the defining steps that adolescents take in establishing their role identity, fulfilling their vision of their role in society.

It is also an area where parents frequently have strong opinions. But if a parent tries to bludgeon an adolescent into accepting a particular college, the issue can shift from what is the best, most suitable school to who has power over whom.

In the end, the parent can refuse to pay for college unless it is the college the parent wants. But that tactic invariably backfires. The adolescent may painfully go along at first, but the odds are that before long he will drop out of school, profoundly angry with his parents and alienated from them.

The unconscious motives of parents are often at the heart of confrontations over college. Without realizing it, the father or mother—usually the father—has strongly invested his own identity and ambitions in the child. The child must perform according to the parent's needs and fantasies.

Relinquishing control

This process can be painful for a loving parent. Nevertheless, it is a critical development, especially if one accepts the thesis that parents are caretakers, with the responsibility to lead their children toward an independent life, one in which they can think and act on their own and take care of themselves.

Relinquishing control is best achieved gradually, throughout the high school years and especially during the years from sixteen to eighteen. To do it, it helps to think ahead to a time when your child has completed high school and become self-sufficient, or is in college. By that point, you want to be reasonably comfortable, trusting that your child can take care of himself fairly well, that he can and will use reasonably good judgment.

Creating a transitional year can smooth the process from adolescent to young adult. The year from age seventeen to eighteen, commonly the last year of high school, is a good time to try to be as uncontrolling as possible, when you try to treat your adolescent as a young adult, when you encourage her to be self-directing.

One of the effects of lessening control is that it should mean fewer severe conflicts over the role-identity issues that surface around this time, like the choice of a college or a career.

Parental control often becomes an issue when adolescents choose boyfriends or girlfriends of whom the parents do not approve. There might be a difference in religion, color, class, or simply a clash of personalities.

Ultimately, the way the relationship evolves between the developing adolescent and his parents depends on the ability of parents to face and live with the inevitable. It depends on the parents' being able to see their adolescent as a young adult.

Getting help

An adolescent can be extremely resistant to accepting the suggestion from her parents that she needs help with her problems, for such an admission would conflict with her push for independence. She is resistant even when she knows she is having serious problems and feeling down about herself; perhaps her grades have dropped, and she has withdrawn from friends and social activities.

To have gone to her parents to talk, to have sought their guidance and comfort, would have been something of a betrayal of her struggle. It would have seemed to her like an admission that she was not strong enough to be independent. It would have meant giving in to the very authority figures from whom she was trying to separate.

In addition, given the process of adolescent upheaval through which she is passing, her own thoughts can begin to seem somewhat questionable, even crazy to her. She may at times question just how solid she is mentally, and the parental suggestion that she indeed needs help can sound like an accusation, that she is in fact crazy. That can obviously be quite terrifying, perhaps even mean that her independence will be controlled. Crazy people, after all, are subject to controls.

Her perspective can change if the problems she is facing are cast as problems of the whole family. She is obviously having difficulties at school, has withdrawn from friends and her parents for whatever reasons. Those conditions affect the whole family. One member of the family cannot be going through such a rough time without affecting the others. They all need guidance.

That approach removes the stigma from the adolescent. No one is pointing a finger at her, accusing her of being crazy, telling her that she needs a psychiatrist.

Once she can overcome her denial and resistance and admit that she is facing problems, problems that may indeed affect the rest of her family, she will usually go with her parents for help.

AGES EIGHTEEN AND ABOVE

Depression

Recent studies indicate that the incidence of depression is increasing among young adults between the ages of eighteen and twenty-two. It is characterized by a depressed or irritable mood that lingers through most of the day, more days than not over a period of a year. Other official symptoms include poor appetite or overeating, insomnia or hypersomnia (oversleeping), low energy or fatigue, low self-esteem, poor concentration or difficulty making decisions, feelings of hopelessness.

Problems in concentrating can lead to difficulties with schoolwork. Without intervention, that can soon cause the depressed individual to flunk subjects, become more unhappy, perhaps even drop out of school and become still more unhappy.

Desperation over helplessness can lead to antisocial flailing, experimenting with drugs, petty vandalism, or sexual promiscuity, all of which can be ways of crying out for help. Any symbolic loss like failing an exam or breaking up with a boyfriend or girlfriend can trigger deeper depression, even mutterings of suicide. A bad divorce in which the adolescent is shuttled between one parent and another can also trigger significant depression.

If you see that your child has a significant drop in grades and is not eating well and not sleeping well and saying things like "Sometimes I want to kill myself," you have a cluster of warnings that you should have your child assessed by a professional.

Common college problems

In my experience, one of the most widespread problems among young college men is depression that sets in after rejection by a woman. I have seen a certain amount of such depression among women as well, but by and large this is much more prevalent among men around the ages of eighteen and nineteen. Though no one is sure why, women seem to respond with less devastation, appear better able to handle these breakups.

Often these are the most intense relationships the young men have had. They are not high school flings, which are often limited by the general standards and practices of high school. For example, it's commonly believed that after high school, life starts anew, that everyone who goes off to college will meet all kinds of new people, and that old ties essentially end with high school graduation.

In college, of course, many of the old protective limitations are removed. You are now solely responsible for what you do. There is no parent around to tell you when to be home. Even the law declares you an adult. So the possibility of a truly serious relationship becomes greater.

When that first adult relationship comes apart—when she tells him, sorry, this is a mistake—it is a blow. And if the young man is shaky in his self-esteem, the blow can be quite shattering. Perhaps he has gone through life requiring feedback from others, especially his parents, to feel secure in his feelings about himself; then the occasion when the woman in his life seems to demean him is traumatic.

Depression sets in. That affects his ability to study, his desire to work. Everything slides, and quite frequently, with students I have counseled, a semester is lost before they feel strong enough to function well.

Depression is also a common problem among workaholics, who were called the "grinds" in my day. They deprive themselves of all pleasures in an obsessive, compulsive, punishing quest. Eventually, depression seeps in. They are so unfulfilled in so many ways, doing nothing but studying, they become miserable and lose their driven focus. They study less efficiently and then begin to panic. When they come to see me, they are panting, "I'm going to flunk out of college! I'm going to flunk out!"

I find this syndrome especially common among medical school students. And once we work a bit in psychotherapy, it's apparent that they are very angry. They talk for the first time of the awful sacrifices they made to get to medical school, and now that they've made it, they're still making those sacrifices, and they don't like medical school. They hate it. (The first and second years of medical school, to be sure, can be remarkably boring.)

As we dig a little deeper, it becomes clear that they are lonely and unsatisfied: they haven't had a date in six months, or they haven't had sex, or anything that's been pleasurable, in six months. And they don't feel they can change their miserable lives.

I can help them understand their anger and see that some balance is possible. Often we trace their feelings back over years, and what we find is that they have established unrealistic expectations for themselves, not that they are responding to driven parents and parents' expectations. They have done it to themselves.

Role identity and parental frustrations

During this time, the late adolescent becoming a young adult is much concerned with the choices and decisions connected with role identity, that expression of the role they see themselves holding in society as adults. These involve the choice of a career, the selection of a job, the choice of a mate.

Among loving parents there is a natural instinct to want to directly influence, if not to completely shape and manage, the process of role identity. But there are healthy limits to how much a parent can do.

In general, this is the worst possible time for parents to pressure their older adolescents. While the young adult is wrestling with these large issues, the parents should be relinquishing control. By now, the young person is usually well into her struggle for independence and so most likely to resent and resist interference with her life. Pressure at this time can poison relationships and fuel rebelliousness.

Even if your adolescent makes a career choice that worries you, most likely she will make her own correction if she discovers for herself that the choice was a mistake. But only after making the discovery herself will she accept it.

Certainly as a loving parent, you want to spare her all pain. But that is not always possible or always best in the end.

I find a common tendency among parents toward overprotectiveness, which is not surprising. But there's a limit to how much parents can do, and probably should do, to shield their adolescent from the blows of society. If there is a recession, for example, and a college graduate cannot find an appealing job, there is nothing his parent can do about the recession. All a parent can do in the face of a profound shift in society is to be supportive and offer help.

Furthermore, overprotectiveness can be a weapon in a parent's unconscious campaign to control an adolescent. In that case, the true motivation is not so much to shield the child as it is to suppress the child.

Parental awareness of tendencies toward overprotection will make the final stages of role identification and selection much smoother and healthier.

Cults

When an adolescent, usually a college student, joins the Moonies or Hare Krishna or an extremely devout religious group, he appears to be striking a radical blow for independence. Normally, such a step is a dramatic divergence from his family and past.

But in the cases I've handled, it has been clear that the opposite is happening. These are young adults who still have profound dependency needs. Though their act separates them from their families, they are really acquiring another family. They are even acquiring another parental figure, since these cults are usually led by a strong individual.

Rather than nurturing independence, cults, of course, insist on narrowly defined conformity. Indeed, it is the tight structuring of life that attracted the young adults I worked with, so insecure were they about themselves.

In one of these cases, the young man turned to a fundamentalist religious cult in the South when, a couple of years into college, his world seemed to crack.

He had been a good high school basketball player, imagined himself becoming a college star and then going on to fame and glory in the pros. He never was that good, as he was beginning to see in college when a knee injury stopped him from playing. Without basketball, he appeared to be robbed of part of his identity.

Then, while he was recuperating, another fantasy of his was shattered. Although he imagined himself becoming a great and popular writer, his college professors increasingly disagreed. He was not admitted to the honors writing program, and another slice of identity was erased.

The young man could not cope with the shattering of these fantasies and had something of a breakdown. He began to fail courses and drifted into a Bible cult. Apparently, it offered him a tenuous hold on life.

His parents turned to me for guidance, and I had to tell them that there wasn't much that could be done unless their son was willing to see a therapist.

They went south, talked with him and the dean of his college, and were able to steer the young man to the college clinic. Actually, they were helped by the head of the cult, who was growing frightened of the fellow, who was now hearing voices and seeing visions.

For eighteen months, he received intensive therapy and medication and became more stable. He remained in the cult, got involved with a young woman from the group but started to live a life apart from it. Eventually, the two of them married and left the cult. He never finished college, but the last I heard, he had gotten a job in the town, and he and his wife were building a life of their own.

Among other problems, the young man never had an ego that was rooted in reality and strong enough to withstand severe blows. Great disappointments are painful for us all but do not send most of us reeling into a cult, do not send us turning to a group that will repair our lives for us. We still have the strength to confront the blows and make the repairs ourselves. We have an inner sense of identity that supports us.

I have seen this desperate search for identity played out in similar if less extreme ways with adolescents who leave their families and the traditional paths and drift into ashrams or, in a few cases I'm familiar with, into kibbutzim in Israel.

In all these cases, the young adults seemed to feel that they had not lived up to expectations. It was not clear whether these were expectations actually projected by their parents or expectations they had conceived in their own minds and imposed on themselves. They felt like failures, and their search was a way of proving themselves. They were searching for a new identity because the one they had did not satisfy them, and they did not seem to be able to make less radical adjustments.

What do I mean by "less radical adjustments"? Consider some common responses of candidates to medical school when I ask them what they will do if they don't get accepted. "I'll get my Ph.D. and go into research," they'll say, or "I'll get my Ph.D. in psychology and become a therapist." In other words, they do not have their identities so heavily invested in being a doctor that anything else would be an ego-crushing and disabling blow. They are not driven by overpowering needs to please their parents or to fulfill unrealistic goals.

Extended adolescence

In recent years, largely because of the weak economy, a growing number of older adolescents, young adults really, have found themselves blocked. They have completed college and are ready to take the next great step in their lives, one that will bring them financial independence and usually complete their adolescence. But they have been unable to find the jobs they want and so have been thrown back on their parents, forced to remain dependent, to endure an extended adolescence.

It is a profound jolt for them and their parents as well, who were anticipating a new stage in their own lives, a time when they would be relieved of many of their parental burdens. For both, it is a highly stressful situation, a turn in life that is full of traps.

The young adult faces the loss of freedom he knew in his life away at college, and a shattering loss of self-esteem from the rejection of being turned down for the job he wants.

His parents, meaning well, nevertheless quite typically revert unconsciously to their old pattern of setting the rules, which is infantilizing and further demoralizing for the older adolescent.

Life under those circumstances is a daily strain for everyone and potentially explosive. One of the best solutions to this problem is for the parents, where possible, to subsidize their child so he can live elsewhere, outside the family home.

That step immediately removes tension and friction. The young adult is not subjected to infantilizing treatment; independence is preserved, self-esteem restored. In addition, his sexual life remains private, rather than a huge issue for the entire family.

If the expense of a separate living arrangement is prohibitive and the young adult must live at home, there are ways of respecting his needs for separation and privacy. Perhaps a small studio with its own entrance can be created in the basement of the house. Or, with apartments, a back room can be remodeled to provide a semblance of privacy. If the young adult is working, I think it is best for everyone if he pays some rent, even if it's only a token amount. He can then feel like a contributing adult, and his self-esteem will be lifted.

Generally, parents can play a critical role in their older adolescent's recovery. They can empathize with the psychological blow he has suffered and, without infantilizing him, show and tell him that they do understand.

They can be honestly encouraging. They can encourage him to pursue his basic ambitions and not take the first job he's offered, simply because it is a job.

And when the job he wants does come along, if it pays less than expected, they can offer to subsidize his career for a while, reminding him that it is still an opportunity to get started in the field of his choice, and it is a great accomplishment that he was chosen for it. It is hard to overestimate what a profound ego lift such a supportive response can be.

Index